READ ALOUD Anthology

McGRAW-HILL MATHEMATICS

GRADE 3

Math in my World

McGraw-Hill School Division
New York Farmington

Covers for the Read-Aloud Anthologies show details of fabric art created by the Kuna Indians of Panama. Called Molas, these brilliantly colored designs are stitched appliqued panels traditionally used to decorate women's clothes.

McGraw-Hill School Division
A Division of The McGraw-Hill Companies

McGraw-Hill School Division
1221 Avenue of the Americas
New York, New York 10020

Printed in the United States of America
ISBN 0-02-109566-3 / 3
6 7 8 9 024 03 02 01 00

ACKNOWLEDGMENTS

The publisher gratefully acknowledges permission to reprint the following copyrighted material:

"Age" by Avelyn Davidson from the UNDERSTANDING MATHEMATICS series. Reprinted by permission of Shortland Publications Limited.

"Big Business," Chapter 3 from MAX MALONE MAKES A MILLION by Charlotte Herman. Copyright © 1991 by Charlotte Herman. Reprinted by permission of Henry Holt and Co., Inc.

Excerpt from CITY GREEN by DyAnne DiSalvo-Ryan. Copyright © 1994 by DyAnne - DiSalvo-Ryan. By permission of Morrow Junior Books, a division of William Morrow & Company, Inc.

"The Difference" from ARITHMETIC IN VERSE AND RHYME by Allan and Leland Jacobs. Copyright © 1971 by Allan and Leland Jacobs. Reprinted by permission of Allan Jacobs.

8,000 STONES: *A Chinese Folktale* by Diane Wolkstein. Text copyright © 1972 by Diane Wolkstein. Reprinted by permission of the author.

"Enty Merchants, Erith Robbers," from QUICK WITS AND NIMBLE FINGERS by Bernice Wells Carlson. Illustrated by Dolores Marie Rowland. Copyright © 1979 by Abingdon Press. Used by permission.

Excerpt from FLAT STANLEY by Jeff Brown. Text copyright © 1964 by Jeff Brown. Used by permission of HarperCollins Publishers.

Excerpt from GARAGE SALE FEVER by Laurie Meyers. Text copyright © 1993 by Laurie Meyers. Used by permission of HarperCollins Publishers.

"Guno's Hunger" from KANTCHIL'S LIME PIT AND OTHER STORIES FROM INDONESIA by Harold Courlander. Copyright © 1950, 1978 by Harold Courlander. Reprinted by permission of the Estate of Harold Courlander.

"I'm Good at Naming" by Lee Blair from ARITHMETIC IN VERSE by Allan and Leland Jacobs. Copyright © 1971 by Allan and Leland Jacobs. Reprinted by permission of Allan Jacobs.

"Indians of the Plains Say..." from AMERICAN INDIANS SING by Charles Hoffmann. Copyright © 1967 by Charles Hoffmann. Reprinted by permission of HarperCollins Publishers.

"It's Hot...Really! Treasure of a Desert Park" by Judith Reynard. Copyright © WORLD magazine, December 1995. Reprinted with permission of National Geographic WORLD, the official magazine for Junior Members of the National Geographic Society.

"Kate 'n Toady: Collection Day" by Lissa Rovetch from SPIDER magazine, April 1995. Copyright © 1995 by Lissa Rovetch. Used with permission.

Excerpt from MUSIC, MUSIC FOR EVERYONE by Vera B. Williams. Copyright © 1984 by Vera B. Williams. By permission of Greenwillow Books, a division of William Morrow and Company, Inc.

NINE-IN-ONE, GRR! GRR! told by Blia Xiong, adapted by Cathy Spagnoli. Text copyright © 1989 by Cathy Spagnoli. Reprinted with permission of Children's Book Press, San Francisco, CA.

(continued on page 72)

CONTENTS

Young Lions
a story by Toshi Yoshida 1

The Number of Spots
an African folktale from *The Long Grass Whispers*
retold by Geraldine Elliot 3

City Green
a selection by DyAnne DiSalvo-Ryan 7

Guno's Hunger
an Indonesian folktale retold by Harold Courlander 11

Garage Sale Fever
a selection by Laurie Myers 13

The Difference
a poem from *Arithmetic in Verse and Rhyme*
selected by Allan and Leland Jacobs 15

Flat Stanley
a selection by Jeff Brown 16

Age
a poem by Avelyn Davidson 18

Music, Music for Everyone
a story by Vera B. Williams 19

Practicing
a poem by Sandra Liatsos 23

Kate 'n Toady: Collection Day
a selection by Lissa Rovetch 24

I'm Good at Naming
a poem by Lee Blair 26

It's Hot . . . Really! Treasures of a Desert Park
an article by Judith E. Rinard
from *National Geographic World* 27

Nine-In-One Grr! Grr!
a Laotian folktale told by Blia Xiong,
adapted by Cathy Spagnoli 29

The Two Foolish Cats
a Japanese folktale retold by Yoshiko Uchida 32

Enty Merchants, Erith Robbers
an Indian folktale adapted by Bernice Wells Carlson 37

The Race That Was Rigged
a Swazi story from *When Hippo Was Hairy and Other Tales from Africa*
told by Nick Greaves 40

8,000 Stones
a Chinese folktale retold by Diane Wolkstein 43

The Village of Round and Square Houses
an African folktale by Ann Grifalconi 47

Indians of the Plains Say
a Native American poem selected by Flora Hood 53

Totem Pole
a nonfiction selection by Diane Hoyt-Goldsmith 54

Tom Fox and the Apple Pie
a story by Clyde Watson 55

The Twelve Circus Rings
a story by Seymour Chwast 58

Riddle 14
a Mexican riddle from *Mother Goose on the Rio Grande*
selected by F. Alexander, H. M. Hunnicutt, B. Acevedo, and H. Ramirez 61

Big Business
a selection from *Max Malone Makes a Million* by Charlotte Herman 62

Index 66

USING THE ANTHOLOGY

This chart correlates the Anthology selections to the 1998 Grade 3 *Math in My World* program. Chapter number in boldface indicates where the selection is used in the Teacher's Edition of the program.

SELECTION	PAGE	CHAPTER
Young Lions (a story by Toshi Yoshida)	1	**1**
The Number of Spots (an African folktale from *The Long Grass Whispers* retold by Geraldine Elliot)	3	**1**
City Green (a selection by DyAnne DiSalvo-Ryan)	7	**2**
Guno's Hunger (an Indonesian folktale retold by Harold Courlander)	11	**2**
Garage Sale Fever (a selection by Laurie Myers)	13	**3**
The Difference (a poem from *Arithmetic in Verse and Rhyme* selected by Allan and Leland Jacobs)	15	**3**
Flat Stanley (a selection by Jeff Brown)	16	**4**
Age (a poem by Avelyn Davidson)	18	**4**
Music, Music for Everyone (a story by Vera B. Williams)	19	**5**
Practicing (a poem by Sandra Liatsos)	23	**5**
Kate 'n Toady: Collection Day (a selection by Lissa Rovetch)	24	**6**
I'm Good at Naming (a poem by Lee Blair)	26	**6**
It's Hot . . . Really! Treasures of a Desert Park (an article by Judith E. Rinard from *National Geographic World)*	27	**7**
Nine-In-One Grr! Grr! (a Laotian folktale told by Blia Xiong, adapted by Cathy Spagnoli)	29	**7**
The Two Foolish Cats (a Japanese folktale retold by Yoshiko Uchida)	32	**8**
Enty Merchants, Erith Robbers (an Indian folktale adapted by Bernice Wells Carlson)	37	**8**
The Race That Was Rigged (a Swazi story from *When Hippo Was Hairy and Other Tales from Africa* told by Nick Greaves)	40	**9**
8,000 Stones (a Chinese folktale retold by Diane Wolkstein)	43	**9**
The Village of Round and Square Houses (an African folktale by Ann Grifalconi)	47	**10**
Indians of the Plains Say (a Native American poem selected by Flora Hood)	53	**10**
Totem Pole (a nonfiction selection by Diane Hoyt-Goldsmith)	54	**11**
Tom Fox and the Apple Pie (a story by Clyde Watson)	55	**11**
The Twelve Circus Rings (a story by Seymour Chwast)	58	**12**
Riddle 14 (a Mexican riddle from *Mother Goose on the Rio Grande* selected by F. Alexander, H. M. Hunnicutt, B. Acevedo, and H. Ramirez)	61	**12**
Big Business (a selection from *Max Malone Makes a Million* by Charlotte Herman)	62	**12**

YOUR STUDENTS COULD BECOME

Published Writers!

McGraw-Hill School Publishing Company is seeking original student work to be included in an upcoming Student Math Anthology.

Students may submit original songs, poems, rhymes, and riddles related to mathematics for possible inclusion in this publication.

Check our Resource Village on our Website at
http://www.mmhschool.com
for more information and details!

YOUNG LIONS

by Toshi Yoshida

On their first hunt, three young lions learn that they have a great deal to learn from Father and Mother Lion before they can survive on their own.

Under a shady tree a pride of lions rests from the hot African sun. Some nap peacefully, while small cubs play at their sides. But three young lions are restless.

Their mother is napping, too. Tired of chasing games and hide and seek, they decide to set out on their first hunt alone.

On a nearby hill Father Lion sits on a sun-warmed rock. This is his territory.

Although he does not move, his eyes follow the young lions as they start across the grassy plain.

On their way they see a rhinoceros mother with her baby. Tick birds rest on her back. The lions do not go any closer. Rhinoceroses cannot see well, but their noses and ears are keen.

The wanderers come upon a herd of water buffaloes. At their feet are cattle egrets feeding unafraid of the larger animals. The buffaloes stare at the young lions as they quietly move through the grass.

In a wide field a group of zebras has gathered. The three young lions hide themselves in the deep brush and try to get as close to the zebras as they can.

But the alert zebras see the hiding lions, and the entire herd runs off through the trees.

Suddenly, a herd of impalas dashes across the plain. Something is chasing them!

In the antelope family impalas are among the fastest at running away. The lions crouch and watch as the impalas run and leap past them.

Now two cheetahs come flying by at lightning speed, chasing the impalas. The lions could never run that fast.

Cheetahs are good hunters and good runners, but they cannot run for very long. This time the impalas will not be caught.

Out on the open plain, the lions come upon a flock of vultures eating a dead zebra.

A lone hyena snarls at them. He wants the zebra, too, but there are too many vultures and he backs away.

Across the plain, the young lions see a large herd of animals. As they draw closer, they see that the animals have horns like cows and manes like horses. They are gnus.

Now big sister lion wanders away from the other two lions She makes a wide circle to the far side of a forest. The other lions crouch down and little by little creep closer to the herd of gnus.

Suddenly a gnu dashes away. She has caught the scent of the young lions.

Then the entire herd rushes away from the forest toward the plains. The baby gnus keep up, running as fast as their parents.

With their black manes flying, the gnus run away from the young lions.

Big sister lion runs after the gnus, but she cannot catch up with them.

The gnus disappear far away in a cloud of dust. The young lions now know how hard hunting is. Even for strong, grown-up lions more animals escape than are caught. The sound of the gnus' feet dies away. The grassy plain is silent again.

The lions wander on as evening comes. Now the sun settles behind Mt. Kilimanjaro.

Herds of elephants and giraffes, antelopes and water buffaloes graze on grass and trees.

At night, the lions creep into a jungle. It is dark and quiet. Suddenly, a sharp screech echoes through the trees. High up in the branches of a dark tree, two eyes are staring at them. It is a leopard. He has caught an antelope.

Startled by the leopard, the three young lions start home. On their way, they see a strange animal that curls up into a prickly ball as they surround it.

Little brother paws at the animal, but draws back as the porcupine's needles prick his paw. The lions leave the porcupine and continue home.

As they approach their own territory, they see Mother Lion waiting for them.

The young lions run to her and lick her.

They are glad to be home.

MAKING THE MATH CONNECTION

Ask students:

- If there are 11 lions under the tree at the start of the story, how many are left after the 3 young lions leave?

The Number of Spots

from *The Long Grass Whispers*
by Geraldine Elliot

Who can blame Nyalugwe, the Leopard, for being so vain about his beautiful spots? But it's one thing to admire Leopard's spots and another to count them. This African folktale lends itself to activities in multiplication, addition, estimation, and counting.

Nyalugwe, the Leopard, gazed at his reflection in the Looking-Pool above the waterfall and told himself for the hundredth time that his coat was truly magnificent. Those spots . . . yes, they really were superb!

Suddenly the stillness of the pool was broken as an ugly, flat head appeared above the surface. In alarm, Nyalugwe jumped back. He had not expected to find a Crocodile there—not that N'gona was likely to take liberties with *him,* but, well, you never could tell with Crocodiles.

"Ha!" barked N'gona nastily. "Gazing at yourself as usual, I see. Vain creature!"

"You'd be vain if you'd been given the lovely spots that I have," replied Nyalugwe with dignity.

"Spots–pah! Who wants spots? What's the good of spots I'd like to know."

"You'd soon find out if you lived in the woods instead of in the river."

"The river's a very good place, thank you—or it would be if you didn't come here so often to gaze at your silly self." Crocodile snorted. "I wonder you don't count your precious spots! Or perhaps you have? How many of the pretty things are there?" he enquired with a sneer.

"I don't know. I never thought of counting," said Leopard as he turned the idea over in his mind and found it good. "Now that you have suggested it, I should very much like to know. But I don't see how I can count them for myself." Nyalugwe wasn't going to admit that he did not know how to count, and he wondered if, by any chance, Crocodile knew.

"Would you like to count them for me?" he asked.

"No, I would not!" barked N'gona. "I've something better to do than to waste my time counting spots." And with a vicious swirl of his tail, Crocodile turned and slipped beneath the surface of the water.

"I bet that means N'gona can't count," chuckled Nyalugwe as he stalked up the river bank and wandered into the woods, where he happened to meet Njiri, the Wart-hog.

"Morning, Njiri!" he called out. "I suppose you wouldn't care to count my spots for me, would you?"

"What, me? Count? One-two-three-four?"

"Yes, that's it," cried Leopard excitedly. "What luck that you know how!"

"But I don't," said the surprised Wart-hog. "Whatever made you think that?"

"Oh, you do! You must! . . . what you said—'one-two-something-something.' That's counting."

Wart-hog shook his head.

"It's much more difficult than that," he said earnestly. "There are things that come after 'four,' and I don't know what they are, or what they mean."

"A pity," sighed Nyalugwe, looking very disappointed. "I wonder who would know?"

"Ask at the Drinking-pool to-night," suggested Njiri. "There's sure to be someone there who could help you."

"That's an idea." Nyalugwe brightened up at once. "I know! I'll give a prize to anyone who can tell me how many spots I've got."

There was quite a large gathering at the Drinking-pool that night, and when the animals heard that Nyalugwe was offering a bag of maize as a prize, they were only too eager to start counting. Njobvu, the Elephant, insisted that he should have first try, as he was the oldest and biggest animal present.

"One-two-three-four-five-six-seven-eight-nine-ten," he started, all in one breath and at a tremendous pace. Then he took another breath. "One-two-three-four-five-si . . ."

"No, no!" shrieked the other animals. "You've already got as far as ten." Elephant frowned.

"I should be obliged if you would refrain from interrupting," he said coldly. "You have made me forget where I was . . . somewhere in the second ten, I think?"

"What d'you mean, 'the second ten'?" demanded Nchefu, the Eland.

"The numbers that come after the first ten, of course. I don't approve of those 'teen'-things and I prefer to count ten twice, which makes twenty. It's all a Question-of-Multiplication." Njobvu's air of superiority was quite insufferable, and although none of the animals knew what Elephant meant by this last remark, they were determined not to be impressed.

"Supposing you start again at the beginning," suggested Njati, the Buffalo.

So Elephant began again, and when he'd counted ten twice and made it twenty he stood quite still and thought so hard that his whole face puckered up into little wrinkles. Then, slowly, he made his announcement.

"Nyalugwe has *more* than twenty spots."

"How many more?" asked Leopard.

Again Njobvu frowned.

"A good many more, I should say"—his manner was exceedingly casual. "In fact, there are so many that I haven't time to count them for you, and really I must be going." With a condescending nod he began to walk away, looking exactly as if he had an important appointment to keep, though of course he hadn't, and there was no need whatever for him to go.

"Tee-hee!" giggled a young Bushbuck. "I don't believe Elephant can count above twenty for all the airs he gives himself!" (And Bushbuck was quite right.)

"Can *you* count above twenty?" asked Leopard, but not very hopefully.

"Me?" Oh, no! I can only count four. I can do that because I know I've got four legs."

Nyalugwe sighed. He was beginning to feel depressed.

"Can't *anyone* count better than Elephant?" he asked sadly.

"I once counted up to fifty," said Nkaka, the Ant-bear, diffidently. "Do you think that would be enough?"

"It might. Come and try."

"Very well. Where shall I start? At the tail, I think . . . one, two, three, four, five . . . now I wonder if that ought to count as one or two spots? It's sort of double."

All the animals crowded round and looked at the spot in question. After a good deal of arguing, it was agreed that it should only count as one.

"What does that make, then?" asked Nkaka.

"Six," said Jackal.

"Five—Nkaka said"—this from Eland.

"Better start again," said Njati, the Buffalo, in a mournful voice.

Nkaka took his advice and got as far as eleven without any trouble. "... twelve ... that's a very fine spot, that is! ... twelve ..."

"You've said 'twelve' once," muttered Eland.

"Sh! Don't interrupt!"

"Oh, dear, you've put me off," complained Nkaka. "Did I count that spot or did I not?"

"Better start again," said Njati gloomily.

Nkaka sighed and did so. This time, with some difficulty, she got as far as twenty-nine. Then she paused and thought hard for a long time.

"It's no good," she said at last. "I've forgotten what comes after twenty-nine."

"Doesn't 'thirty'?" said Kamba, the Tortoise. "Or is it 'forty'?"

"Thirty! That's right!" exclaimed Nkaka joyfully. "Thirty ... now, where was I?"

"Half way up the tail."

"Yes, but was that the twenty-ninth ... or that?" She indicated two spots and a great deal of arguing followed.

"You'll have to start again." Njati, the Buffalo, was almost beginning to enjoy himself.

"Start what again?" It was Kalulu, the Rabbit, who spoke. He had only that moment arrived and knew nothing of what was going on.

Instantly all the Animals began to talk at once and explain about Leopard's spots.

"Wants to know how many he's got, does he?" said Kalulu when he had, at last, managed to grasp what they were trying to say. "Well, that oughtn't to be difficult. I can tell him."

"You can?"

"Yes. It's easy. Look?" Kalulu pointed to the first spot. "This one is dark, isn't it?" Now, *this* one is light. Here ... dark ... here ... light ... dark ... light ... dark ..." He went on until every spot had been touched.

"You see?" he said when he had finished. "Leopard has only got two spots—dark ones and light ones."

CITY GREEN

by DyAnne DiSalvo-Ryan

This story depicts what happens when Marcy and her neighbors decide to turn an ugly lot into a beautiful garden. The transformation of Old Man Hammer is even more amazing than that of the garden.

Marcy feels sad because the building that Old Man Hammer used to live in was torn down and now an ugly lot stands in its place. She and Miss Rosa, with the help of their neighbors, decide to lease the lot from the city to plant their own private garden.

Saturday morning I'm up with the sun and looking at this lot. My mama looks out too. "Marcy," she says, and hugs me close. "Today I'm helping you and Rosa."

After shopping, Mama empties her grocery bags and folds them flat to carry under her arm. "Come on, Mrs. B.," Mama tells her friend. "We're going to clear this lot."

Then what do you know but my brother comes along. My brother is tall and strong. At first, he scratches his neck and shakes his head just like Old Man Hammer. But Mama smiles and says, "None of that here!" So all day long he piles junk in those bags and carries them to the curb.

Now, this time of day is early. Neighbors pass by and see what we're doing. Most say, "We want to help too." They have a little time to spare. Then this one calls that one and that one calls another.

"Come on and help," I call to Old Man Hammer.

"I'm not helpin' nobody," he hollers. "You're all wastin' your time."

Sour grapes my mama'd say, and sour grapes is right.

Just before supper, when we are good and hungry, my mama looks around this lot. "Marcy," she says, "you're making something happen here."

Next day the city drops off tools like rakes and brooms, and a Dumpster for trash. Now there's even more neighbors to help. Miss Rosa, my brother, and I say "Good morning" to Old Man Hammer, but Old Man Hammer just waves like he's swatting a fly.

"Why is Old Man Hammer so mean and cranky these days?" my brother asks.

"Maybe he's really sad," I tell him. "Maybe he misses his building."

"That rotten old building?" My brother shrugs. "He should be happy the city tore down that mess."

"Give him time," Miss Rosa says. "Good things take time."

Mr. Bennett brings wood—old slats he's saved and nails in a cup. "I knew all along I saved them for something," he says. "This wood's good wood."

Then Mr. Rocco from two houses down comes, carrying two cans of paint. "I'll never use these," he says. "The color's too bright. But here, this lot could use some brightening up."

Well, anyone can tell with all the excitement that something is going on. And everyone has an idea about what to plant—strawberries, carrots, lettuce, and more. Tulips and daisies, petunias, and more! Sonny turns the dirt over with a snow shovel. Even Leslie's baby tries to dig with a spoon.

For lunch, Miss Rosa brings milk and jelly and bread and spreads a beach towel where the junk is cleared. By the end of the day a fence is built and painted as bright as the sun.

Later, Mama kisses my cheek and closes my bedroom door. By the streetlights I see Old Man Hammer come down his steps to open the gate and walk to the back of this lot. He bends down quick, sprinkling something from his pocket and covering it over with dirt.

In the morning I tell my brother. "Oh, Marcy," he says. "You're dreaming. You're wishing too hard."

But I know what I saw, and I tell my mama, "Old Man Hammer's planted some seeds."

Right after breakfast, I walk to the back of this lot. And there it is—a tiny raised bed of soil. It is neat and tidy, just like the rows we've planted. Now I know for sure that Old Man Hammer planted something. So I pat the soil for good luck and make a little fence to keep the seeds safe.

Every day I go for a look inside our garden lot. Other neighbors stop in too. One day Mrs. Wells comes by. "This is right where my grandmother's bedroom used to be," she says. "That's why I planted my flowers there."

I feel sad when I hear that. With all the digging and planting and weeding and watering, I'd forgotten about the building that had been on this lot. Old Man Hammer had lived there too. I go to the back, where he planted his seeds. I wonder if this was the place where his room used to be.

I look down. Beside my feet, some tiny stems are sprouting. Old Man Hammer's seeds have grown! I run to his stoop. "Come with me!" I beg, tugging at his hand. "You'll want to see."

I walk him past the hollyhocks, the daisies, the peppers, the rows of lettuce. I show him the strawberries that I planted. When Old Man Hammer sees his little garden bed, his sour grapes turn sweet. "Marcy, child." He shakes his head. "This lot was good for nothin'. Now it's nothin' but good," he says.

Soon summertime comes, and this lot really grows. It fills with vegetables, herbs, and flowers. And way in the back, taller than anything else, is a beautiful patch of yellow sunflowers. Old Man Hammer comes every day. He sits in the sun, eats his lunch, and sometimes comes back with supper.

Nobody knows how the sunflowers came—not Leslie, my brother, or Miss Rosa. Not Mr. Bennett, or Sonny, or anyone else. But Old Man Hammer just sits there smiling at me. We know whose flowers they are.

STARTING A COMMUNITY GARDEN

All across America people have joined together to turn ugly lots into beautiful gardens. You may not imagine that you can do it—but you can. If there is already a community garden in your neighborhood, ask your neighbors how they got started. But if you are the first on your block to "make something happen," this is what you can do:

1. Find an interested grown-up who wants to help you: a parent or guardian, a teacher, a librarian, or a neighbor.
2. Find out the address of the lot. This is very important. You may have to talk to neighbors or look at the address of the buildings next door. Example: The lot I am interested in is on Main Street. It is between 75 Main Street and 81 Main Street.
3. While you are finding out the address of the lot, get in touch with the local gardening program in your area (see end of this note). Say that you are interested in starting a garden. Since every city is different, your local program will be able to steer you in the right direction.

4. Find out who the owner is. The Department of Records at your local city hall can help. Look in the telephone book for the address of city hall in your area.
5. If the lot is owned by the city, the people at city hall can help you get permission to use the lot. Usually there is a small fee. If the lot is owned by an individual person or group, you will need to get permission from that person or group to use the lot.
6. Once you get permission to use the lot, it's yours to name.

There are hundreds of gardening programs that are ready to help community gardeners with information, soil, seeds, fencing, and more.

To find out the community gardening program that is nearest you, write to

American Community Gardening Association
325 Walnut Street
Philadelphia, PA 19106

Community gardens bring people together. Join the work and join the fun!

MAKING THE MATH CONNECTION

Ask students:

- Each box of seeds bought for the garden holds 10 bags. If Marcy has 3 boxes, how many bags of seeds does she have?
- Marcy counts 36 daisies and 27 hollyhocks. Which plant are there more of?

GUNO'S HUNGER

by Harold Courlander

Although his name means "useful" or "helpful" in the Malayu language of Sumatra, Guno never lives up to it. His foolish behavior is the basis for many stories.

Guno, the "helpful one," went one day from his village to Macassar to sell some knives he had made. He knew he wouldn't be home again before night, so he asked his wife for six rice cakes to feed him during thc day. He walked briskly toward the city, but before the sun had risen high in the sky he was already hungry.

Guno sat in the shade of a large tree and looked at his rice cakes. He knew it was too early to eat, and that he must save his food for later in the day. But he was hungry, and he argued with himself. Finally he took one cake and ate it. But he was still hungry.

"Well, I will take one more and save four for the evening," he said to himself.

He took one more. But he was still hungry. So he ate the third.

Then he stopped arguing with himself, and he ate the fourth rice cake. Then the fifth.

There was only one left. Guno looked at it longingly, for he was still hungry. At last he said: "Ah, let the evening take care of itself!"

And he put the last cake in his mouth and ate it. When he had eaten it he discovered that he was no longer hungry. His stomach was completely satisfied.

He looked into his empty basket and said:

"Oh, how foolish I was! Now there is nothing more to eat. It was the *sixth* rice cake that stopped my hunger. If I had only eaten the sixth one first, then my selfish stomach would have stopped its complaints immediately, and I would have had five cakes left for the evening."

Garage Sale Fever

by Laurie Myers

Will thought he saw a two-headed monster peering through his bedroom window, but it was really the heads of two of the many women who had come to his garage sale!

There was a strange ringing going on and on. Will turned over in his bed. His eyes had not yet opened.

"Will, get the door! I'm sure it's for you," his mother yelled. "Somebody for the sale."

Will opened his eyes. What he saw scared him so badly he almost screamed. There were two faces peering through his bedroom window. It looked like a two-headed monster. One head was big and lumpy, while the other was small and round with big shiny eyes.

Will blinked to see better. The window was smudged from Leo's nose. He blinked again. The picture came in clear. It was two women, one with glasses, and one with her hair in rollers. The lady with rollers had a scarf pulled around her head and tied in the back. It was a bad attempt to hide the rollers. Will blinked again and they were gone.

. . .

He went out the kitchen door and into the garage. There were seven or eight faces pushed up against the glass windowpanes in the garage door. Two of them belonged to the two-headed monster. Will reached down and pulled the door up. Immediately the people came in and moved quickly from one table to the next, like bumblebees moving from flower to flower.

"Hey, we've got customers already!" Pete said, pulling his wagon up the drive. It was loaded with more items for the sale. One of the ladies started searching the wagon before it came to a complete stop. Pete stood by, shaking his head.

"I didn't think anyone would come," he said. "And look. There are one, two, three . . ." He began counting the customers. "Nine," he said, pointing to the woman going through his wagon. "Nine people and it's only"—he looked at his watch—"seven forty-five! This is great."

One lady pulled a vase from the wagon. "How much do you want for this?" she asked.

"Four dollars," Pete said.

"Will you take three?" she asked.

This was Pete's first time bargaining. He glanced at Will.

"How about three fifty?" Pete replied.

She pulled out her wallet. "Okay."

As Pete was taking the money and removing the sticker, another car pulled into the driveway.

"Do you have any old records?" A man stuck his head out the window without getting out of his car.

"No," Will answered. The man backed out and was gone.

Pete set up the cashier's table while Will got out two lawn chairs to sit on. The chairs were old, and the webbing was torn and hanging off in places. Only a couple of strips were left on the seats.

"How much do you want for those?" a man asked.

"They're not for sale," Will answered.

"Those aren't in the sale?" Pete asked in disbelief. "They're junk. Pure junk."

"These are our Leo chairs," Will answered.

Leo walked over and sat beside the chairs. He reached up, took a loose strip of webbing in his mouth, and started chewing.

"Some things are not for sale at any price," Will said. He scratched Leo's head.

Pete sat down on the seat, carefully positioning himself to the right to avoid falling through a large hole.

Will and Pete spent the next two hours at the table taking money from a steady stream of customers. Some spent only a quarter, and some spent as much as fifteen dollars. Will and Pete's kindergarten teacher came by and bought the large Legos for her class. Even Mrs. Hamilton came by. She bought the exercise jump rope.

By ten o'clock the crowd had thinned out and there was only an occasional customer.

MAKING THE MATH CONNECTION

Ask students:

- Pete sold a vase for \$3.50 and a jump rope for \$1.75. How much money does he have?

THE DIFFERENCE

from *Arithmetic in Verse and Rhyme*
selected by Allan and Leland Jacobs

What is the difference between a penny and a dime? The teacher in this poem may expect an answer such as "A penny is larger than a dime," but Dennis has subtraction on his mind!

What is the difference,
Dear Dennis,
Dear Dennis,
Between a penny and a dime?

This is the difference,
Dear Teacher,
Dear Teacher:
Exactly nine cents every time!

Anonymous

Flat Stanley

by Jeff Brown

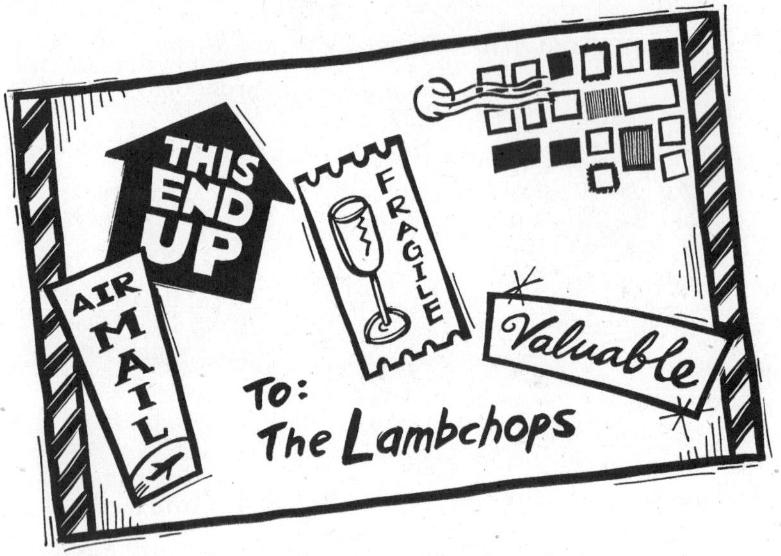

Mr. Lambchop devised a unique way to send Stanley to visit his friend in California.

One day Stanley got a letter from his friend Thomas Anthony Jeffrey, whose family had moved recently to California. A school vacation was about to begin, and Stanley was invited to spend it with the Jeffreys.

"Oh, boy!" Stanley said. "I would love to go!"

Mr. Lambchop sighed. "A round-trip train or airplane ticket to California is very expensive," he said. "I will have to think of some cheaper way."

When Mr. Lambchop came home from the office that evening, he brought with him an enormous brown-paper envelope.

"Now then, Stanley," he said. "Try this for size."

The envelope fit Stanley very well. There was even room left over, Mrs. Lambchop discovered, for an egg-salad sandwich made with thin bread, and a toothbrush case filled with milk.

They had to put a great many stamps on the envelope to pay for both airmail and insurance, but it was still much less expensive than a train or airplane ticket to California.

The next day Mr. and Mrs. Lambchop slid Stanley into his envelope, along with the egg-salad sandwich and the toothbrush case full of milk, and mailed him from the box on the corner. The envelope had to be folded to fit through the slot, but Stanley was a limber boy, and inside the box he straightened right up again.

Mrs. Lambchop was nervous because Stanley had never been away from home alone before. She rapped on the box.

"Can you hear me, dear?" she called. "Are you all right?"

Stanley's voice came quite clearly. "I'm fine. Can I eat my sandwich now?"

"Wait an hour. And try not to get overheated, dear," Mrs. Lambchop said. Then she and Mr. Lambchop cried out, "Good-bye, good-bye!" and went home.

Stanley had a fine time in California. When the visit was over, the Jeffreys returned him in a beautiful white envelope they had made themselves. It had red-and-blue markings to show that it was airmail, and Thomas Jeffrey had lettered it "Valuable" and "Fragile" and "This End Up" on both sides.

Back home Stanley told his family that he had been handled so carefully he never felt a single bump. Mr. Lambchop said it proved that jet planes were wonderful, and so was the Postal Service, and that this was a great age in which to live.

Stanley thought so too.

MAKING THE MATH CONNECTION

Ask students:

- An airline ticket to California costs $376. It costs $68 to mail a package the size of Stanley. How much money did Stanley's parents save?

Have students compare the cost of traveling by airplane to sending a package to somewhere they would like to go.

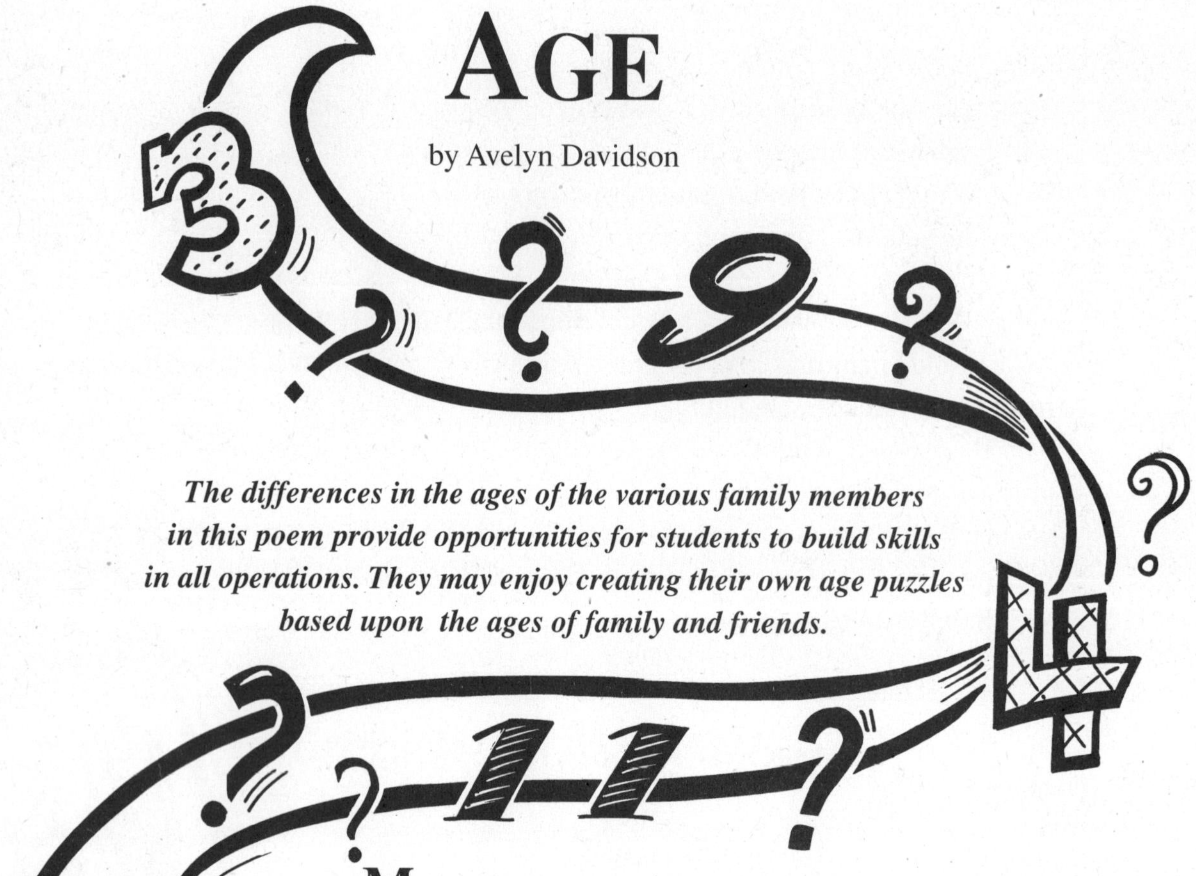

AGE

by Avelyn Davidson

The differences in the ages of the various family members in this poem provide opportunities for students to build skills in all operations. They may enjoy creating their own age puzzles based upon the ages of family and friends.

Mary's five and Bea is three,
Bob is nine, that's three times Bea.
In four more years I'll be eleven,
That's much better than being seven.
Grandad's sixty I was told,
How many years till I'm that old?
Funny how Mum's age never changes,
She's been twenty-one for ages.

Music, Music for Everyone

by Vera B. Williams

Because Grandma feels better when she hears Rosa and her friends play their musical instruments, Rosa decides to form a band. When Leora's mother invites them to play at a family party, Rosa is delighted to see her Grandma smiling and keeping time by tapping her cane.

Our big chair often sits in our living room empty now.

When I first got my accordion, Grandma and Mama used to sit in that chair together to listen to me practice. And every day after school while Mama was at her job at the diner, Grandma would be sitting in the chair by the window. Even if it was snowing big flakes down on her hair, she would lean way out to call, "Hurry up, Pussycat. I've got something nice for you."

But now Grandma is sick. She has to stay upstairs in the big bed in Aunt Ida and Uncle Sandy's extra room. Mama and Aunt Ida and Uncle Sandy and I take turns taking care of her. When I come home from school, I run right upstairs to ask Grandma if she wants anything. I carry up the soup Mama has left for her. I water her plants and report if the Christmas cactus has any flowers yet. Then I sit on her bed and tell her about everything.

Grandma likes it when my friends Leora, Jenny, and Mae come home with me because we play music for her. Leora plays the drums. Mae plays the flute. Jenny plays fiddle and I play my accordion. One time we played a dance for Grandma that we learned in the music club at school.

Grandma clapped until it made her too tired. She told us it was like the music in the village where she lived when she was a girl. It made her want to dance right down the street. We had to keep her from trying to hop out of bed to go to the kitchen to fix us a treat.

Leona and Jenny and Mae and I left Grandma to rest and went down to get our own treat. We squeezed together into our big chair to eat it.

"It feels sad down there without your grandma," Leora said. "Even your big money jar up there looks sad and empty."

"Remember how it was full to the top and I couldn't even lift it when we bought the chair for my mother?" I said.

"And remember how it was more than half full when you got your accordion?" Jenny said.

"I bet it's empty now because your mother has to spend all her money to take care of your grandma till she gets better. That's how it was when my father had his accident and couldn't go to work for a long time," Mae said.

Mae had a dime in her pocket and she dropped it into the jar. "That will make it look a little fuller anyway," she said as she went home.

But after Jenny and Leora and Mae went home, our jar looked even emptier to me. I wondered how we would ever be able to fill it up again while Grandma was sick. I wondered when Grandma would be able to come downstairs again. Even our beautiful chair with roses all over it seemed empty with just me in the corner of it. The whole house seemed so empty and so quiet.

I got out my accordion and I started to play. The notes sounded beautiful in the empty room. One song that is an old tune sounded so pretty I played it over and over. I remembered what my mother had told me about my other grandma and how she used to play the accordion. Even when she was a girl not much bigger than I, she would get up and play at a party or a wedding so the company could dance and sing. Then people would stamp their feet and yell, "More, more!" When they went home, they would leave money on the table for her.

That's how I got my idea for how I could help fill up the jar again. I ran right upstairs. "Grandma," I whispered. "Grandma?"

"Is that you, pussycat?" she answered in a sleepy voice. "I was just having such a nice dream about you. Then I woke up and heard you playing that beautiful old song. Come. Sit here and brush my hair."

I brushed Grandma's hair and told her my whole idea. She thought it was a great idea. "But tell the truth, Grandma," I begged her. "Do you think kids could really do that?"

"I think you and Jenny and Leora and Mae could do it. No question. No question at all," she answered. "Only don't wait a minute to talk to them about it. Go call and ask them now."

And that was how the Oak Street Band got started.

Our music teachers helped up pick out pieces we could all play together. Aunt Ida, who plays guitar, helped us practice. We practiced on our back porch. One day our neighbor leaned out his window in his pajamas and yelled, "Listen, kids, you sound great but give me a break. I work at night. I've got to get some sleep in the daytime." After that we practiced inside. Grandma said it was helping her get better faster than anything.

At last my accordion teacher said we sounded very good. Uncle Sandy said so too. Aunt Ida and Grandma said we were terrific. Mama said she thought anyone would be glad to have us play for them.

It was Leora's mother who gave us our first job. She asked us to come and play at a party for Leora's great-grandmother and great-grandfather. It was going to be a special anniversary for them. It was fifty years ago on that day they first opened their market on our corner. Now Leora's mother takes care of the market. She always plays the radio loud while she works. But for the party she said there just had to be live music.

All of Leora's aunts and uncles and cousins came to the party. Lots of people from our block came too. Mama and Aunt Ida and Uncle Sandy walked down from our house very slowly with Grandma. It was Grandma's first big day out.

There was a long table in the backyard made from little tables all pushed together. It was covered with so many big dishes of food you could hardly see the tablecloth. But I was too excited to eat anything.

Leora and Jenny and Mae and I waited over by the rosebush. Each of us had her instrument all ready. But everyone else went on eating and talking and eating some more. We didn't see how they would ever get around to listening to us. And we didn't see how we could be brave enough to begin.

At last Leora's mother pulled us right up in front of everybody. She banged on a pitcher with a spoon to get attention.

Then she introduced each one of us. "And *now* we're going to have music," she said. "Music and dancing for everyone."

It was quiet as school assembly. Every single person there was looking right at Leora and Jenny and Mae and me. But we just stood there and stared right back. Then I heard my grandma whisper, "Play, Pussycat. Play anything. Just like you used to play for me."

I put my fingers on the keys and buttons of my accordion. Jenny tucked her fiddle under her chin. Mae put her flute to her mouth. Leora held up her drums. After that we played and played. We made mistakes, but we played like a real band. The little lanterns came on. Everyone danced.

Mama and Aunt Ida and Uncle Sandy smiled at us every time they danced by. Grandma kept time nodding her head and tapping with the cane she uses now. Leora and Jenny and Mae and I forgot about being scared. We loved the sound of the Oak Street Band.

And afterward everybody clapped and shouted. Leora's great-grandfather and great-grandmother thanked us. They said we had made their party something they would always remember. Leora's father piled up plates of food for us. My mama arranged for Leora, Jenny, and Mae to stay over at our house. And when we finally all went out the gate together, late at night, Leora's mother tucked an envelope with our money into Leora's pocket.

As soon as we got home, we piled into my bed to divide the money. We made four equal shares. Leora said she was going to save up for a bigger drum. Mae wasn't sure what she would do with her share. Jenny fell asleep before she could tell us. But I couldn't even lie down until I climbed up and put mine right into our big jar on the shelf near our chair.

MAKING THE MATH CONNECTION

Ask students:

- If the girls practice from 3:45 to 5:30, for how long do they practice?
- What would you do to raise money if you wanted to?

Have students use the data to make a class graph or line plot.

Practicing

by Sandra Liatsos

Students may enjoy creating and illustrating their own poems about the things they would like to count.

I'm counting cats
who cross my path.
I'm counting dogs
and birds.
I'd rather be counting
buffalo
that run in furry herds.

I'm counting rocks
beside my feet.
I'm counting
telephone poles.
I'd rather be counting
down in the lake
nice, wriggly, black tadpoles.

Kate 'n Toady: Collection Day

by Lissa Rovetch

Kate couldn't come up with a collection that she really cared about until she had a wonderful idea. She named it her "Friend Collection."

"WHAT A TERRIBLE idea!" said Kate. "Whoever thought of having a collection day?"

"I did," said Toady. "And it's a great idea! Everyone's going to love my rock collection."

"Who cares about a bunch of dumb old rocks?" said Kate.

"You're just jealous because you don't have a collection," said Toady.

"I could have a collection if I wanted to," said Kate.

"Well, here's some granite," said Toady. "Just in case you decide to collect rocks."

Kate put the rock in her basket and went to visit Charlie, who was working on his baseball-card collection.

"Isn't that kind of boring?" asked Kate.

"Are you kidding?" said Charlie. "If you don't collect baseball cards, you shouldn't collect anything."

"What's so great about baseball cards?" asked Kate.

"Everything!" said Charlie. "You've got your uniforms, and your hits, and your career totals. What could be better than that?"

Charlie gave Kate an extra card, and she walked across the street to Penny's house.

"Isn't this collecting thing just plain silly?" said Kate.

"It sure is!" said Penny. "Unless, of course, you happen to collect hair bows."

"How many hair bows do you have?" asked Kate.

"Sixty-five," said Penny. "Any time I have a birthday or anything, I just ask for hair bows."

"You mean that's all you ever get?" asked Kate.

"Sometimes I get other things," said Penny. "But I never like them as much. Once you find something that you really, really care about, that's when you're ready to have a collection."

"I don't think I care about anything as much as you care about hair bows," said Kate.

"I have two with unicorns," said Penny. "You can take one and start your own hair-bow collection."

Kate thanked Penny and headed back home. On her way she bumped into Betsy Potter.

"You always know everything, Betsy," said Kate. "If somebody needed to collect something, what would you suggest?"

"Collection day is tomorrow!" said Betsy. "Do you mean to say that you haven't even started your collection yet?"

"Not exactly," said Kate. "I haven't quite decided which one of my collections I like best."

"Is one of them an elephant collection?" asked Betsy.

"It might be," said Kate.

"Then that's the one you should choose," said Betsy. "I have an elephant box, and some elephant socks, and about a zillion other elephant things. I had a cousin from China once who had a berry collection. That was a pretty good idea. Except they got all smushy, and his mom threw them away because they had to go back to China, and you can't take smushy berries on the airplane."

"How come I've never met this cousin?" asked Kate.

"The important thing," said Betsy, "is that we elephant collectors stick together. So you can take my extra elephant magnet."

Kate spent the rest of the day thinking. As hard as she tried, she still couldn't come up with a collection that she really, really cared about. But the next morning, when everybody met on Crab Apple Hill, Kate got an idea. She asked all her friends for one thing from their collection. Soon her basket was filled to the top.

"Look, everybody!" she said. "Each thing in this basket reminds me of someone I really, really care about. I guess you could call it my friend collection."

"Don't you mean your friend-and-brother collection?"asked Toady.

"Oh, Toady," said Kate. "Don't you know that you're my friend, too?"

MAKING THE MATH CONNECTION

Ask students:

- Toady has 5 types of rocks. He has 4 rocks of each type. How many rocks does he have? How did you find the total?

I'm Good at Naming

by Lee Blair

Eyes and ears, hands and feet (and mittens and shoes) come in two's, but what comes in three's? Your students may enjoy writing their own poems about things that come in sets.

I'm good at naming
Things in two's,
Like slippers, mittens,
Socks, and shoes,
Like eyes and ears
Or arms and knees,
Or hands on clocks,
And things like these.

But will you kindly
Help me, please,
With things that always
Come in three's?

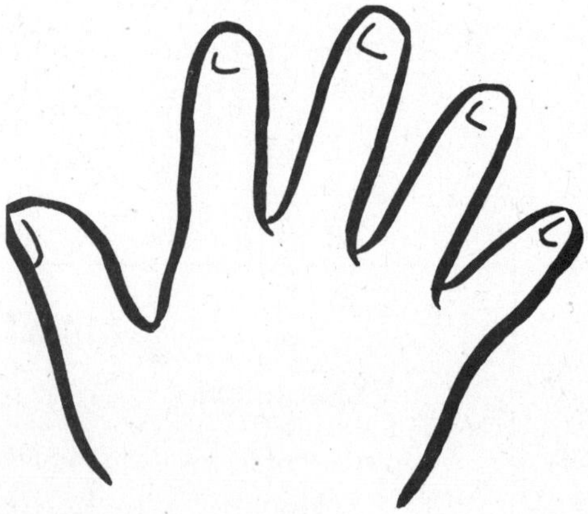

IT'S HOT . . . REALLY!

Treasures of a Desert Park

by Judith E. Rinard

This magazine article invites the children to explore exciting Saguaro National Park, which boasts numerous giant plants.

It's the only national park on two sides of a major city. It's also one of the newer national parks in the United States. Which one is it? Saguaro National Park—and the city it straddles is Tucson, Arizona.

The park is named for the saguaro (suh-WAH-ro), the largest cactus in the country. You can see lots of these giant plants in the park, which covers 90,000 acres of the Sonoran Desert. The park protects not just the saguaro, but the community of desert life around the plant.

Birds, mice, coyotes, and ants eat the saguaro's flowers. Some birds make their homes inside the plants. Bees, bats, and other birds help pollinate them.

The park is full of life in spite of dry, scorching heat—more than 100°F in summer. To learn more, read on.

You're in for a surprise if you think that a desert is nothing but bare land. The Sonoran Desert is one of the hotter and drier of North American deserts, "but it has by far the most diverse wildlife," says Stan Lawhead, a ranger at Saguaro National Park.

The desert park swarms with life. Many kinds of cactus besides the saguaro grow here. Other desert plants bloom in bright colors. The plants store water and can survive months without rain. Desert animals are adapted to life with little rain, too. They often stay in the shade or underground during the hottest part of the day.

Some come out only in the brief summer rainy season.

If you expect a desert to be flat, you're in for another surprise. Parts of the Sonoran Desert inside the park range from the low-lying desert floor to mountains 9,000 feet high. In the cooler mountain climate, plants and animals not thought of as desert dwellers thrive. Forests of pine trees grow, and black bears roam.

Both sections of the park—east and west of Tucson—have trails, visitor centers, and scenic drives. Hikers may come across pictures scratched into rocks by the Hohokam—prehistoric Indians.

Kids can earn a Junior Ranger certificate and badge at the park. To do so, they hike in the desert and learn to identify plants, animals, and animal tracks. And they may spot—at a safe distance—roadrunners, jackrabbits, and coyotes. If you visit the park, you'll agree with Ranger Lawhead. He says "It's an exciting place to explore."

MAKING THE MATH CONNECTION

Ask students:

- If the ranger guides 8 tour groups a day and there are 6 people in each group, how many people does he guide each day?
- Write a problem about a national park that can be solved using multiplication.

NINE-IN-ONE GRR! GRR!

A Folktale from the Hmong People of Laos
told by Blia Xiong and adapted by Cathy Spagnoli

This Laotian folktale originates from the Hmong (Mong) people in the mountains of Laos. "Nine-in-one," Tiger sings, imagining the nine cubs she will have every year. But Bird's interruption changes the song, and Tiger begins singing, "One-in-nine," imagining the one cub she will have every nine years.

Many years ago when the earth was nearer the sky than it is today, there lived the first tiger. She and her mate had no babies and so the lonely tiger often thought about the future, wondering how many cubs she would have.

Tiger decided to visit the great god Shao, who lived in the sky, who was kind and gentle and knew everything. Surely Shao could tell her how many cubs she would have.

Tiger set out on the road that led to the sky. She climbed through forests of striped bamboo and wild banana trees, past plants curved like rooster tail feathers, and over rocks shaped like sleeping dragons.

At last Tiger came to a stone wall. Beyond the wall was a garden where children played happily under a plum tree. A large house stood nearby, its colorful decorations shining in the sun. This was the land of the great Shao, a peaceful land without sickness or death.

Shao himself came out to greet Tiger. The silver coins dangling from his belt sounded softly as he walked.

"Why did you come here, Tiger?" he asked gently.

"O great Shao," answered Tiger respectfully, "I am lonely and want to know how many cubs I will have."

Shao was silent for a moment. Then he replied. "Nine each year."

"How wonderful," purred Tiger. "Thank you so much, great Shao." And she turned to leave with her good news.

"One moment, Tiger," said Shao. "You must remember carefully what I said. The words alone tell you how many cubs you will have. Do not forget them, for if you do, I cannot help you."

At first Tiger was happy as she followed the road back to earth. But soon, she began to worry.

"Oh dear," she said to herself. "My memory is so bad. How will I ever remember those important words of Shao?" She thought and she thought. At last, she had an idea. "I'll make up a little song to sing. Then I won't forget." So Tiger began to sing:

Nine-in-one, Grr! Grr!
Nine-in-one, Grr! Grr!

Down the mountain went Tiger, past the rocks shaped like sleeping dragons, past the plants curved like rooster tail feathers, through the forests of striped bamboo and wild banana trees. Over and over she sang her song:

Nine-in-One, Grr! Grr!
Nine-in-One, Grr! Grr!

As Tiger came closer to her cave, she passed through clouds of tiny white butterflies. She heard monkeys and barking deer. She saw green-striped snakes, quails and pheasants. None of the animals listened to her song—except one big, clever, black bird, the Eu bird.

"Hmm," said Bird to herself. "I wonder why Tiger is coming down the mountain singing that song and grinning from ear to ear. I'd better find out." So Bird soared up the ladder which was a shortcut to Shao's home.

"O wise Shao," asked Bird politely, "why is Tiger singing over and over:

Nine-in-one, Grr! Grr!
Nine-in-one, Grr! Grr!"

And Shao explained that he had just told Tiger she would have nine cubs each year.

"That's terrible!" squawked Bird. "If Tiger has nine cubs each year, they will eat all of us. Soon there will be nothing but tigers in the land. You must change what you said, O Shao!"

"I cannot take back my words," sighed Shao. "I promised Tiger that she would have nine cubs every year as long as she remembered my words."

"As long as she remembered your words," repeated Bird thoughtfully. "Then I know what I must do, O great Shao."

Bird now had a plan. She could hardly wait to try it out. Quickly, she returned to earth in search of Tiger.

Bird reached her favorite tree as old grandmother sun was setting, just in time to hear Tiger coming closer and closer and still singing:

Nine-in-one, Grr! Grr!
Nine-in-one, Grr! Grr!

Tiger was concentrating so hard on her song that she didn't even see Bird landing in the tree above her.

Suddenly, Bird began to flap her wings furiously. "Flap! Flap! Flap!" went Bird's big black wings.

"Who's that?" cried Tiger.

"It's only me," answered Bird innocently.

Tiger looked up and growled at Bird: "Grr! Grr! Bird. You made me forget my song with all your noise."

"Oh, I can help you," chirped Bird sweetly. "I heard you walking through the woods. You were singing:

One-in-nine, Grr! Grr!
One-in-nine, Grr! Grr!

"Oh, thank you, thank you, Bird!" cried Tiger. "I will have one cub every nine years. How wonderful! This time I won't forget!"

So Tiger returned to her cave, singing happily:

One-in-nine, Grr! Grr!
One-in-nine, Grr! Grr!

And that is why, the Hmong people say,
we don't have too many tigers on the earth today!

The Two Foolish Cats

by Yoshiko Uchida

Two hungry cats find a large rice cake and a small rice cake. The two hungry cats become two greedy cats as they fight over who should receive the larger cake. At last they seek advice on how to divide the cakes fairly. The solution of the wise old monkey of the mountains leaves the two cats hungry – and foolish.

Long ago, at the edge of a dark pine forest in Japan, there lived two cats named Daizo and Suki. Because Daizo was big and fierce and had seven toes on each paw, he was called Big Daizo. Because Suki was small and skinny, he was called Little Suki.

When the field mice saw Big Daizo swishing his tail and stalking through the tall grass, they ran to hide in their tiny holes. They were afraid of Big Daizo, for they knew he could pounce on them with his seven-toed paws and swallow them in one gulp for dinner.

The birds of the forest were afraid of Little Suki, for they knew that if he caught them, he would surely gobble them down in a minute.

The two cats got on quite well and hunted together each day in the meadows and streams. One spring morning when the snow had melted from the mountains and the meadows were turning green, they went out to catch some field mice for breakfast. They hunched low in the tall grass, waiting and watching, silent and still.

But the field mice saw the two cats waiting for them.

"Not for anything will we go out today," they whispered, and they huddled safe in their cozy nests.

Soon Little Suki grumbled, "Those field mice are never coming out. Let's go catch some fish instead."

So the two cats raced as fast as they could to the stream at the edge of the meadow.

Big Daizo plunged first into the icy water. SPLATT! SPLASH! He pounced on a silvery trout. But the fish was much too fast for him. It shimmered and slipped away swiftly down the mountain stream.

"You are much too slow," Little Suki scoffed. "You must be quick and clever like me. Watch!"

And Little Suki jumped into the stream, his sharp claws spread, his whiskers twitching. SPLATT! SPLASH! He pounced, quick as lightning. But today, the speckled trout were too fast even for him.

"You're not so fast after all," Big Daizo complained. "You didn't catch a single fish."

"Well, neither did you," Little Suki hissed.

"Eowrrrrr," the cats growled, glaring at each other.

They sat at the edge of the stream, wet and hungry. Just when they had decided to give up and go home, they saw two rice cakes in the tall reeds nearby. One was big and plump, but the other was very small.

"Look!" Little Suki shouted. And because he was faster, he got to the rice cakes first.

"I'll take the big one," he said, "because I'm small and skinny and need more food to grow on."

"Oh no you don't!" Big Daizo hissed. "I should have the biggest rice cake because I need more food than you do. Give it to me at once!"

"No!" Little Suki shouted. "The big one is mine!"

"You are not only skinny and scrawny," Big Daizo screeched, "you are stubborn and greedy as well!"

Soon the two cats were snarling and spitting at each other. They clawed and scratched, they hissed and yowled, and they chased each other around and around the trees.

The field mice looked out from their holes and watched the cats fight.

"Banzai! Hooray!" they squealed. "Maybe they will eat each other up and leave us alone."

The blue jays and mockingbirds flew down to see what the racket was all about.

"Look! Look!" they cried. "The two cats are fighting. They are so greedy and stubborn, they will never stop."

Soon the old badger hurried out from the forest.

"Stop your yowling and screeching," he scolded. "You are making so much noise, you will awaken the Thunder God in the sky, and then he will tilt the rain barrels and pour rain on all our heads!"

Since Big Daizo and Little Suki were growing weary, they stopped snarling long enough to tell the badger about the two rice cakes.

"All that racket over two silly rice cakes?" the old badger asked. "Go find the old monkey of the mountain," he told the cats. "He is clever and wise and he will settle your quarrel. He will see that you get equal shares."

"That is a fine idea," the two cats agreed, for by now they wanted to stop fighting and eat their rice cakes.

So Big Daizo and Little Suki hurried through the pine forest, heading toward the mountain where the wise old monkey lived. They followed curving paths that wound through the trees. They climbed over logs and under curtains of moss. They crossed a marsh and scrambled through thick vines. Finally, they stopped for a drink at a deep mountain pool.

"Garrump . . . garrump . . ." the great frog who guarded the pool called out to them. "What brings you cats to my mountain pool?"

"We are going to see the wise old monkey of the mountain," they explained. "Tell us, are we almost there?"

"You must go up and up and around and over, and then up some more," the frog garrumped.

So the two cats hurried on. Up and up and around and over, and up and up some more.

At last they passed through a grove of bamboo and reached the top of the mountain. And there was the wise old monkey, sitting on a tree branch, having a cup of tea.

The two cats held up their rice cakes and both began to talk at once.

"Stop! One at a time!" the old monkey scolded.

So Big Daizo held up the small rice cake and told the monkey why he should have the big one. And Little Suki held up the big rice cake and told why he deserved to keep it.

"Ah *hah,* ah *hah,*" the old monkey said, stroking his chin. "I see your problem and I will solve it for you."

"Thank you, Mr. Monkey," the two cats purred. "We knew you were wiser than anyone in the forest."

The old monkey disappeared into his house and soon returned with a pair of tiny scales. He put one rice cake on each side of the scale, but of course they did not balance.

"Ah *hah,* ha *hah,*" the old monkey said. "I can soon fix that."

And he quickly took a bite from the larger rice cake.

"Now," he said, "they should both be equal."

But he had eaten too much, and now the smaller rice cake was heavier.

"Ah *hah,* ha *hah,* I can soon fix that," the old monkey said. And this time he took a bite from the smaller rice cake.

But of course he had again eaten too much.

"Ah hah, ha hah, I shall soon fix that," the old monkey said once more, and he took still another bite.

"Ah . . . er . . . uh . . . Mr. Wise Monkey, sir," Big Daizo said, twitching his whiskers. "Don't you think you have taken quite enough from each rice cake?"

"Yes, yes," Little Suki agreed. "Surely they must be equal by now."

But the clever old monkey paid no attention to the cats. He just went right on, weighing and munching, weighing and munching, until at last he had eaten up both rice cakes.

Then he looked slyly at the two cats and said, "Well, your rice cakes are now equally gone. I told you I would stop your quarreling and indeed I have. For now there is nothing left for you to quarrel about."

And with a quick flick of his tail, the old monkey took his tiny scales and disappeared into his house.

"Eowrrr . . ." Big Daizo wailed. "I feel foolishly *stupid.*"

And Little Suki wailed, "Eowrrr . . . I feel stupidly *foolish.*"

Above their heads the blue jays laughed and the mockingbirds mocked, "Silleeeee cats! Foooolish cats!" And they flew through the forest telling everyone the tale of the two foolish cats.

When the old badger heard them, he roared with laughter.

"Ha ha, ha ha!
Ho ho, ho ho!
What foolish cats!
Their rice cakes are gone!"

When the mice in the meadow heard the tale, they scrambled out of their holes and danced with joy.

"Ha ha, ho ho,
Ha Ha, hee hee," they sang.
"The wise old monkey
Fooled Daizo and Suki!"

As Big Daizo and Little Suki slunk home quietly, they heard the sounds of laughter echoing all through the forest and fields and far out into the starry skies.

And ever since that day, the two cats never quarreled again, but lived peacefully together at the edge of the dark pine forest.

MAKING THE MATH CONNECTION

Ask students:

- If the 2 cats had 8 small rice cakes instead of the two cakes they had, how could they have shared them equally?
- How could the cats have shared the two cakes equally?

Enty Merchants, Erith Robbers

retold by Bernice Wells Carlson

This folktale from India tells the story of 10 merchants who are outnumbered by 3 robbers. A secret code among the merchants enables them to outwit the robbers. Before reading the story aloud to the students, make a list of the words with which they may not be familiar.

At one point in the story, the robbers make the merchants disrobe down to their loincloths. You may wish to revise the story somewhat or explain to the students that loincloths were articles of underclothing worn several hundred years ago.

Long ago, there lived in India ten cloth merchants who always traveled together. As they worked with each other, they developed a secret code that enabled them to talk in the presence of a buyer without revealing the lowest price at which an item might be sold.

If a buyer refused to pay twenty rupees for a length of cloth, a merchant might ask his partner, "What's our lowest price for this cloth?"

The second merchant might look at the cloth, feel it, consider the matter, act as if he hated to sell the cloth at a loss, and mumble, "Enty rupees," meaning ten rupees.

The buyer, who couldn't understand the secret-code word, might offer fifteen rupees, or some other amount, and purchase the cloth, unless, of course, he offered less than ten rupees. The system worked very well, and the merchants prospered.

As the merchants grew richer, they traveled farther and farther afield, making more and more money on each trip. When they were returning home from one such trip, laden with money and a few remaining bags of merchandise, they came to a cool, inviting forest with one well-traveled path running through it—a pleasant place to walk during the heat of the day.

Down the path the merchants ambled, single file, each enjoying his own dream of what he would do with his new wealth, each completely unaware of the fact that in this forest there lived three notorious robbers.

When the merchants reached the middle of the woods, the three robbers suddenly appeared. With raised cudgels and swords, they ordered the merchants to lay down all they had.

What could the merchants do? They had no weapons. They dropped their bags of money and cloth.

Then the robbers commanded the merchants to undress down to their loincloths.

Still the merchants felt defenseless. One by one, each man disrobed and stood, humiliated, with his fellow traders.

The robbers laughed and laughed, as loud as they could. The sight of the ten pompous men standing huddled together, wearing only loincloths, made them proud. They, three robbers, had overcome ten wealthy merchants, plundered their property, and made them stand near-naked. Why not carry the jest farther, one robber suggested. Treat the stuffy merchants like fools. Make them dance!

"Agreed!" his cohorts said. Whereupon, the three robbers seated themselves regally before the merchants, and raising their swords, ordered them to dance.

Nine of the merchants cowered before the robbers and mourned their fate. They had lost their wealth, even their clothing. They were forced to stand in the presence of other men, wearing only loincloths. Yet the robbers were not satisfied. They commanded them to dance. Why should well-traveled merchants dance like fools before robbers? "Alas! Our fate!" they sighed. "Alas!"

The tenth merchant wasted no time in moaning. He considered the situation carefully, pondering the loss of money and clothing, the dance they no doubt would have to perform, and the arrogant manner in which the robbers had seated themselves on the grass.

The nine merchants began to dance a sluggish shuffle. The robbers jeered at them, and then, placing their weapons on the ground, pulled out bags of betel nuts so they might chew as they enjoyed the spectacle.

At that moment, the tenth merchant dashed away from the group and began to dance with great leaps in a circle around the robbers. As he danced, he sang a strange song in a false voice, like a cry from the distant jungle.

We are enty men.
They are erith men.
If each erith men
Surround eno man,
Eno man remains.
Ta! Tam! Tom! Tadinganna!

The song meant nothing to the robbers, who were watching the leaping leader, not trying to understand the words of his song.

But the nine other merchants got the message. In their code, it meant:

We are ten men.
They are three men.
If each three men
Surround one man,
One man remains
To tie them up!

The nine merchants stopped their sluggish shuffle. They, too, began to leap around the robbers in a large circle. They followed their leader as he invented new rhythms. As the merchants danced, the leader repeated his strange song three times.

The robbers were overcome with laughter. Never had they imagined anything so funny as these ten potbellied merchants . . . shimmying like belly dancers, gyrating like men of the jungle.

The robbers howled, clapped in time to the rhythms, and swayed back and forth as if they were in a trance. The merchants danced on and on, the circle getting smaller and smaller, closer and closer to the robbers.

Suddenly the leader let out on wild, piercing cry—"Owny!" (Now!)

The merchants quickly separated into groups of three. Each group surround a robber and pinned him to the ground. The leader opened a bag, ripped pieces of cloth into strips, and securely bound each robber—feet, arms, and eyes and mouth for good measure. The robbers lay on the ground like three bags of rice.

The merchants lost no time. Hurriedly, they scooped up their clothing, their bags of money and cloth, and the robbers' cudgels and swords. Down the path they fled, until they emerged from the forest, a strange-looking but triumphant group of men.

THE RACE THAT WAS RIGGED

retold by Nick Greaves

This Swazi story from Africa about the tortoise and the hare is a read-aloud selection. You may wish to give synonyms for the words "ponderous," "earnest," and "plodded."

Tortoise was eating peacefully one day, minding his own business, when along came Mofuli, the hare. Mofuli, like all wicked little hares, could not resist the chance to make fun of Tortoise and tease him about how slow and ponderous he was.

Mofuli, full of mischief, challenged Tortoise to a race. There were some palm trees about 550 yards (500 metres) from where they were, and Mofuli said that was where they would race to.

Tortoise had had enough of Mofuli, and all hares, to last him a lifetime, since this was not the first time he had been teased by one of these irritating creatures. He wished he could put Hare in his place once and for all.

He thought for a moment and then said, "Speed is not everything, Mofuli. One must have endurance, too. Let us make this a real race — a long one. Let us race to the Blue Pan, some six miles (ten kilometres) from here. And, so that I have time to prepare, let us run the race in five days' time, at noon."

Mofuli was most surprised. He hadn't expected Tortoise to accept the challenge, and had been looking forward to a good long teasing. But he was scornful, and he almost decided not to bother with the race. But Tortoise was so much in earnest, that in the end he agreed. And Hare went on his way, laughing. He could hardly wait to tell all the other animals about the silly old Tortoise.

But Tortoise lost no time. He called on his relatives for help, telling them about his plan. It was very simple: at noon on Saturday, they were to place themselves in different positions all along the path that Hare and Tortoise were to race. Every one of them was to run toward Blue Pan, starting from different points along the route. All they had to do was to keep going as fast as they could, until Hare had sped past, and then they could go home and rest if they wanted to.

Tortoise collected a gourd to hold water, and set off for the pan that very day. It took him almost five days to get to Blue Pan, but at last he arrived. At noon Saturday, he filled his gourd with water and settled down to wait.

Meanwhile Mofuli had arrived at the starting point at the agreed time, and there he found Tortoise's cousin. It did not occur to Mofuli that this was a different tortoise. They greeted each other, and the race began.

Mofuli was out of sight in a twinkling, and Tortoise's cousin plodded off on his way, chuckling to himself. Mofuli was laughing too, until he reached the first rise and there was Tortoise ahead of him! (Actually, it was Tortoise's brother, stumbling along as fast as he could go.) Mofuli ran faster and soon he was out of sight. He was rather puzzled, and as the race went on, he became more and more confused.

Over each hill, Mofuli found Tortoise in front of him. Each time he overtook him, running like the wind, Tortoise would laugh loudly. By now, Hare was thinking that Tortoise must have learned to fly.

It was very hot, being midday, and the sun beat down. The pan was still two miles (three kilometres) away, and Mofuli was terribly thirsty. He came over the next rise to find Tortoise, ahead of him again!

In desperation, Mofuli put on his last burst of speed. Heart pounding, he strained every muscle, and at last came in sight of the Blue Pan. He was almost at the pan, when suddenly he tripped and fell. He lay on the ground, exhausted — he could go no further. His sides were heaving and every limb was trembling.

After a few moments he staggered to his feet. He looked up and what do you think he saw?

Why, Tortoise, of course, walking towards him from the pan, carrying a gourd of cool, clear water. This sight was more than Mofuli could stand. He fainted from shock and exhaustion.

Tortoise revived Hare by sprinkling cold water over his face. When Mofuli came round, Tortoise said in a soothing voice, "Drink this, my poor friend. I had an idea that you might be needing it. The endurance of some animals is not quite what they claim it to be." And he chuckled quietly to himself.

So it was that slow old Tortoise beat Hare at his own game. Clever as he was, Mofuli did not have the brains to see that he himself had at last been made a fool of.

MAKING THE MATH CONNECTION

Have students plan a race they could run near the school. Then have them estimate the total distance of the race.

8,000 STONES

A Chinese Folktale
retold by Diane Wolkstein

When Ts'ao Ts'ao receives the gift of an elephant, the first ever seen in China, he wants to know how much it weighs. With the help of a toy sailboat, Ts'ao Ts'ao's young son figures out a way to measure the elephant.

Long ago in China, there lived a very powerful ruler. He was known as the Most Supreme Governor of China. His name was Ts'ao Ts'ao.

Ts'ao Ts'ao ruled the royal city of Loyang and lived in a beautiful palace surrounded by lovely gardens. The treasures of the royal city and palace were well protected by the Governor's mighty army of 10,000 soldiers.

But the neighboring kings and princes heard of Ts'ao Ts'ao's beautiful palace and mighty army, and they came themselves or sent messengers to see the wonders of the royal city. The messengers often brought splendid presents.

This year the Satrap, or prince, of India sent Ts'ao Ts'ao a most unusual present: a present that neither Ts'ao Ts' ao nor anyone in Ts'ao Ts'ao's kingdom had ever seen before. When the Indian messengers arrived in Loyang, the peasants came running from their fields to see the marvelous creature. The courtiers came out of the palace, and soon a huge noisy crowd formed around the animal.

Then Ts'ao Ts'ao appeared, and the Indian messengers, the peasants, and all the court knelt before him.

"Rise!" Ts'ao Ts'ao commanded the Indian messengers. "Rise and explain the cause of this uproar. What is this beast doing in my kingdom?"

"It is a present," explained the messengers. "It is a present from the Grand Satrap of India to the Most Supreme Governor of China, Ruler of Loyang, General of 10,000 soldiers—Yourself!"

"Oh . . . oh yes," muttered Ts'ao Ts'ao. (He just then remembered that this was the time of year the Satrap's presents usually did arrive.)

"Delighted!" exclaimed Ts'ao Ts'ao. "The Grand Satrap of India is to be informed that I am delighted with his . . . his . . . what is it called, his . . . ?"

"Elephant!" answered the messengers.

Jumma, the son of one of the Indian messengers, showed his small ivory elephant to P'ei, the son of Ts'ao Ts'ao. P'ei showed Jumma his new Chinese sailboat.

"And how tall is my elephant?" asked Ts'ao Ts'ao.

"Ten feet tall, Most Supreme Governor of China."

"And how much does my elephant weigh?"

"Oh, we cannot tell you Most Supreme Governor. There are no scales in India large enough to weigh such an animal."

"You mean to say that the Grand Satrap of India does not know how much an elephant weighs?"

"That is correct, Most Supreme Governor of China."

"I see," said Ts'ao Ts'ao, "I see . . . ."

When the Indian messengers had been led into the palace to eat and rest, Ts'ao Ts'ao called his advisers together: "I want to know, before the messengers leave at the end of the month, the exact weight of my elephant. If the Grand Satrap of India does not know how to weigh an elephant, then I, Ts'ao Ts'ao, Ruler of Loyang, General of 10,000 soldiers shall show him the way!"

The advisers then spent all their time thinking:

How to weigh an elephant . . . ?

How to weigh the Most Supreme Governor of China's elephant?

How to weigh the elephant?

But they could not think of a way. Then a week before the messengers were to leave, little P'ei came from playing with his sailboat to see the wonderful elephant.

"What are you doing under the elephant?" he called to the advisers.

"Shhh . . . we're thinking."

"What about?" whispered P'ei.

"How to weigh an elephant," the advisers whispered back.

"Well, that's not so hard," said P'ei.

"Not so hard?" cried the advisers.

"No," said P'ei. Follow me, and I'll show you." P'ei led them through the woods to a small pond near the palace. There by the pond was P'ei's new toy sailboat. It looked like any toy Chinese sailboat, except it had a strange line carved into its side.

"Wait here!" cried P'ei and he ran back to the palace.

The advisers picked up the boat. They examined the line carefully. At the side of the line was the Chinese character for elephant.

What did it mean?

The advisers shook their heads. They did not understand.

Little P'ei returned from the palace, carrying Jumma's ivory elephant.

"Watch," he said to the advisers.

He placed the elephant on the sailboat and the boat sank in the water to the carved line.

"You see," P'ei explained, "no matter how many times I sailed Jumma's elephant on my boat, it always weighed the boat down to that line, so I carved his character next to it. If you want to weigh the big elephant, you can do the same thing. And if you need to know the exact weight of the elephant, then pile stones on the boat until the boat sinks to the elephant's character."

"That's it ! That's it!" cried the advisers. "Little P'ei, you've shown us the way."

On the day of the weighing, a large crowd of courtiers and peasants gathered around the shore of the palace lake.

The elephant was led from the fields onto a sturdy barge. Little P'ei and the advisers then stepped into a smaller boat.

Little P'ei was given the honor of carving, just above the water line, the character of the Most Supreme Governor of China's elephant on the barge.

After both boats were brought back to shore, the barge was pushed out again. Many stones were piled on it. It took many, many stones for the barge to sink to the character of the elephant. Can you guess how much the elephant weighed?

The elephant weighed 8,000 stones. A gong was sounded and the announcement made by the court herald:

"The Most Supreme Governor of China's elephant weighs the Most High Amount of 8000 stones!"

The peasants cheered and the courtiers applauded.

The gong rang out again. This time Ts'ao Ts'ao, Most Supreme Governor of China, Ruler of Loyang, General of 10,000 soldiers spoke:

"Let it be known that the plan for the weighing of the Most Supreme Governor of China's elephant was thought of by none other than my own son . . . little P'ei."

The peasants, the advisers, and the courtiers cheered even louder.

"AND let it be written in the court annals," continued Ts'ao Ts'ao, "and a copy be given to the Indian messengers to present to the Grand Satrap of India."

So the story of little P'ei and the weight of the elephant were written out and presented to the Indian messengers to take back to the Satrap. And Ts'ao Ts'ao, Most Supreme Governor of China, then became famous—not only for his beautiful palace and mighty army—but also for the Most Supreme Intelligence of his clever son . . . little P'ei.

In later years, little P'ei became Ts'ao P'ei, EMPEROR OF ALL OF CHINA. That was in A.D. 200, almost 2,000 years ago.

THE VILLAGE OF ROUND AND SQUARE HOUSES

by Ann Grifalconi

This story invites the children to visit a remote village in the hills of the Cameroons in Central Africa. Why do the men live in square houses and the women in round ones in this village that clings to the side of an almost extinct volcano?

It was not until I was almost full-grown and left my village
That I found our village was like no other.
For the men live in SQUARE houses, and the women in ROUND ones!
To me, this seemed the natural order of things. . . .
"But what is it like?" you ask.
I will tell you how it was—and is—for me.
I grew up on my grandmother's farm in the village of Tos

That lies at the foot of Naka Mountain in the Bameni Hills of west Africa.
We planted yams and corn and tobacco
And the finest coffee grown in the Cameroons.
Our village was always happy and peaceful—
A good place for any boy or girl to grow up.
Every evening, after a day of work in the fields—
Uncle Domo and Gran'pa Oma came to our round house for supper.
We children would hurry to put out the low, wooden stool for Gran'pa Oma
(For he was the eldest, and closer to the ancestor spirits).
Then we would unroll the grass mat for Uncle Domo, the next oldest
As was only proper and respectful.
Then we would march into the big round room—
Our bare feet gripping the earthen floor.
The little ones went first, carrying the bowl of heated water and towels
To wash the hands before and after eating.
Then the older ones would carry in the stew,
Spicy and steaming—smelling oh, so good!
And I would come in last bearing the *fou-fou*!
Gran'pa, as the eldest, would always eat first,
Dipping the first three fingers of one hand into the *fou-fou*—
Scooping up a small portion which he dipped *quickly* into the stew bowl,
To flavor each bite with the spicy meat and juices!
Then, in order of age—Gran'ma, Uncle Domo, and sometimes Mama
(If she left the cook fire) would finish their meal in the same way,
And we children would follow last—making sure to leave the bowl clean!
But always *I* would be the one to pound and soften the white cassava root,
To make the *fou-fou* we eat at every meal.
Then Mama would cook the *fou-fou* and beat it 'til it was white and fluffy
And she would pile the food into big bowls with round handles—
Just right for our small hands to hold.
After supper, when the men went back to their square house
To smoke, and talk of farming and fishing and the old days of the hunt,
Gran'pa would leave some tobacco for Gran'ma.
(He knew she liked to smoke it later—when everything was peaceful.)
Then she would sit alone in the moonlight, looking up at the dark slope
Of Naka Mountain, rising high above. . . .
We would squirm and make an answer
And wriggle off those sharp knees
And run to help Mama and Gran'ma Tika prepare the meal to come.
Supper might be fish or rabbit or ground-nut stew or yams—
And there they would sit proudly in their bright robes—
Gran'pa Oma above, seated on his stool, hands on knees—

And Uncle Domo seated below.
Then they would ask to see the children!
One by one we would come forward from the narrow doorway . . .
And one by one, we would be lifted to sit upon those high and bony knees,
And Gran'pa would ask each one of us, "What have you learned today?"
I remember one night I sat beside her—Gran'ma Tika took a last puff
on her pipe
Then pointed with it to the sky above our village.
"You see old Mother Naka smoking so peacefully there?"
I leaned way back and looked up to see old Naka's breath
Rising in lazy puffs of smoke, soft and gray in the night sky.
"And you remember that sometimes in the night
We hear old Naka snoring in her sleep?"
I nodded, pleased that Gran'ma felt I was old enough to notice such things.
"Well, it is by these signs that we know she is content.
Now, we live in peace with Naka and the spirits of our ancestors,
But it was not always so!"
Gran'ma fixed me with a stare
And began to rock with the tale . . .
For she was the best storyteller in the whole village!

"In the days of long, long ago,
The people of this village lived
In houses of any sort, either square or round
It did not matter.

"Then, one peaceful night
Before anyone alive remembers
Old Naka began to groan and rumble
And awoke from a long sleep!

"The villagers were frightened
And ran out of their houses
And hid in the bushes
At the foot of the mountain.

"A great wind came up
And the ancestor spirits in the trees
Cried out to warn them—
Even the rocks began to tremble!

"Suddenly, the black night
Was split open like a coconut!
And a great white burst of light
Rose like the sun!

"Then the voice of our mother Naka
Thundered out over all;
BOOM! BA-BOOM! BA-BOOM!

"And the people cried out to Naka,
And prayed where they were lying down,
Hands pressing the earth, asking:
'What have we done to so anger you?'

"All through the night
Old Naka spoke to them
Shouting her anger to the skies
As red rivers of lava flowed down her sides.

"The morning sun rose
But no one could see him—
The anger of Naka was too great
And ashes and smoke filled the air.

"Finally—
No one remembers when—
Naka spoke no more. . . .

"Slowly—carefully—
The people lifted their heads and looked about:
Everything was covered with ashes—
Even themselves!

"Everyone looked like a gray ghost—
No one knew who stood next to them
Or who came behind. . . .

"So they stood there—
Trembling with fear—
But grateful to be alive:
NAKA HAD SPARED THEM!

"Still covered with ashes—
The men, women, and children
Faced the mountain together
And went back to claim their homes.
"But when they came to the burned-out village,
Only two houses were left standing:
One SQUARE— And one ROUND!

"The people saw the only
These two houses had been spared by Naka
And they wondered to themselves:
'*Why these?* Was it a sign'

"But the village chief had no time
For such questions—
And he called them together:
'We must begin to rebuild our village now!'

"He pointed to the ash-covered people:
'You! TALL GRAY THINGS!
You go live in the SQUARE house!

"'And you! ROUND GRAY THINGS—
Go live in the ROUND house!'

"'And you! SMALL GRAY THINGS over there!
You go pick the small gray stones our of the fields
So we can plant our crops again!'

"And so it was done.
The women lived in the round house with the children
And the women talked and laughed—
Preparing food for everyone.

"The men stayed in the square house
And told each other tall stories
And planted yams and corn
Each day, in the new, rich soil.

"And the children made a game
Out of clearing the fields of small, gray stones
And went swimming and fishing in the long afternoons.

"And no one forgot to thank Naka
For sparing their lives
And giving them back such fine crops
From her good earth."

"And the children? Osa—is it not true
The children still keep the fields clear of little gray stones?
"Yes!" I laughed. "And we still swim and play in the afternoon—
But we bring home the fish we catch for supper,
And we all get together then!"

"Til Naka speaks again!"

MAKING THE MATH CONNECTION

Have students draw a village using as many shapes as they can. Have them name the shapes they use. Then have students talk about why certain shapes are used in houses more than other shapes.

Indians of the Plains Say

from *The Turquoise Horse*
selected by Flora Hood

The Great Plains of the United States are home to many Native Americans including the Plains Cree, Blackfoot, Crow, Mandan, Cheyenne, Osage, Kiowa, and Comanche. As a science connection, help students see the circular aspects in nature, such as the seasons and the water cycle.

Indians of the Plains say,
"Because the drum is round
it represents the whole
universe, and its steady,
strong beat is the pulse,
the heart, throbbing at the
center of the universe.
It is the voice of Wakan-Tanka.
And this sound stirs us and
helps us to understand the
mystery and power of all things."

Totem Pole

by Diane Hoyt-Goldsmith

Children will enjoy meeting David, who lives in Washington State, and has learned how to hunt, fish, and carve from his father, an Indian artist.

My name is David. I live in a small town called Kingston in Washington State. In the summer, I like to hunt for salmonberries and blackberries in the fields near our house.

My brother and I like to look out over Puget Sound, watching for the ferry from Seattle. Sometimes, we spot a pair of eagles flying high overhead. This makes us feel lucky because our family belongs to the Eagle Clan, which is our family group within the Tsimshian (TSIM-shee-an) tribe.

Our father is an Indian. He was brought up by his grandparents in Metlakatla (MET-lah-CAT-lah), on Annette Island in Alaska. He was raised in the old ways and traditions. He learned how to hunt, to fish, and to carve.

In our tribe, a person belongs to the same clan as his mother does. Our mother is not Indian. Her ancestors emigrated to the United States from Europe many generations ago. When I was two years old, she was adopted in a special ceremony by two members of the Eagle Clan in Metlakatla. This makes my brother and me members of the Eagle Clan too.

My father is an artist, a wood-carver. Ever since I was little, I have watched him take a piece of wood and carve a creature from it. Sometimes it is a wolf, sometimes a bear, and sometimes an eagle, the symbol and totem of our clan.

MAKING THE MATH CONNECTION

Ask students:

- The totem pole of the Klallam tribe has 6 figures in it. If David's father has carved 3 figures, what fraction of the totem pole has he carved?
- What other fractions have you seen or used?

TOM FOX AND THE APPLE PIE

by Clyde Watson

Tom Fox loves apple pie. Envisioning a pie cut into sixteenths, eighths, fourths, and then halves, he decides that the best part of a whole pie is the whole pie!

Down at the end of Mulberry Lane, there once lived a family of red foxes. There was Pa Fox and Ma Fox and fourteen little red foxes, all the way down to Tom Fox. (Here is a secret you mustn't pass on: Tom Fox was the greediest and laziest little fox in the family. But he was also the youngest and sweetest, as is so often the case.)

One fine summer morning, Tom Fox woke up early and opened the window to let the sun come in. He poked his nose out the window, and then climbed onto the sill, for the smell of something very sweet was blowing in the wind.

"Apple pie!" he said to himself. "That's what it is!" And he looked toward the village, for the wind came from there. In the distance he could see crazy kites and bright balloons flying high above treetops and rooftops.

He pricked up his ears and heard the faraway sounds of music and dancing and laughter.

"Hey!" he shouted. "Hallo! Help! The Fair is here!"

His thirteen brothers and sisters woke up and they started to shout too.

"The Fair! Whoopee! The Fair is here!"

Tom Fox and his special sister Lou-Lou ran to the hollow tree and pulled out their bag of pennies. Tom tied it to his belt.

"I want a big blue balloon," said Lou-Lou.

"You know what I want?" asked Tom.

But just at that moment, Ma and Pa Fox appeared.

"Breakfast!" said Ma Fox. "Cornbread and Honey!"

"And then out to the garden," said Pa Fox. "There's work to be done."

Poor little fox children! They weeded and watered and hoed and dug all morning long, while the sounds and smells of the fair danced in the wind and teased them with dreams.

But didn't I tell you little Tom Fox was the laziest and greediest fox child of all? Besides, there was nothing he loved better then apple pie. So along about noon, he whispered good-bye to Lou-Lou, sneaked away through the rows of corn, and set off for town sniffing the wind and following his nose.

He hadn't far to go before he saw the striped tops of tents, and the music got louder, the colors brighter, the smells more delicious, and then—there he was in the middle of the fairgrounds. All around him were candy booths and popcorn booths, booths where you could buy apples and cider, ginger cookies and lollipops, to say nothing of booths where you could try your skill and win all sorts of grand prizes. . . . But Tom Fox knew what he wanted, and he headed straight for the apple pie booth.

There he saw tiny apple pies as small as a paw, and big enormous pies the size of Lou-Lou, but Tom settled for a splendid middle-sized pie all brown and crisp and juicy. He counted out twenty-five pennies and the pie lady tied the pie all up in a box. With his last five pennies Tom got a great big blue balloon with a face on it for Lou-Lou. And then, with the box under his arm and the balloon tied to his belt, Tom started off home, hoping to get there before anyone noticed he was gone.

As he walked, he could just see Ma Fox's knife slicing the pie into sixteen pieces, one for everybody, and he hurried even faster toward home. But suddenly he slowed down.

"Feathers and Foxgloves!" he said out loud. "If this poor pie is cut into sixteen pieces, how tiny those pieces will be! Why, they'll be so small, I won't taste the apple part at all!" So he thought. And this is what he came up with:

"Why not wait until Sara and Simon and Sally and Sam, Cyrus and Cissi and Cecily and Celia go out to count the stars tonight. If they're gone, we'll need just eight pieces and they'll be *much* bigger."

"But," he thought as he rounded a bend, "The pieces still won't be all *that* big. Why not stay awake until the others fall asleep, and then Lou-Lou and I will sneak out of bed and tiptoe downstairs with the pie and surprise Ma and Pa! That's only four of us, and four big pieces of pie!"

He stuck his nose in the box. Um-m-m! If only Lou-Lou were there! The two of them could share it, and each take half.

Just then a brown toad hopped across the road.

"What a pity to cut it at all," muttered the toad as he disappeared on the other side.

"Of course!" said Tom. He sat down under the hedge and opened the box, and do you know what?

He ate the WHOLE PIE all by himself.

He was so full when he finished the last bite that he fell fast asleep under the hedge. When he woke up it was dark, and the moon was rising. Now they'd know he was gone for sure! Oh, No!

He ran on home, and puffed in at the door. There sat the whole fox family just finishing a grand supper of beans and carrots fresh from the garden, and not a snip of bean nor the end of a carrot was left for Tom.

"To bed without your supper, you lazy child!" said Ma Fox.

But did Tom Fox care? No sir! His stomach
was warm and full with eating
that fine apple
pie.

THE
H N
END

THE TWELVE CIRCUS RINGS

by Seymour Chwast

Is there a child who does not love a circus? This story teaches children about numbers, multiplication, division, and patterns in a most delightful way.

In the first circus ring, my sister saw with me a daredevil on a high wire.

In the second circus ring, my sister saw with me two elephants and a daredevil on a high wire.

In the third circus ring, my sister saw with me three monkeys playing, two elephants, and a daredevil on a high wire.

In the fourth circus ring, my sister saw with me four aerialists zooming, three monkeys playing, two elephants, and a daredevil on a high wire.

In the fifth circus ring, my sister saw with me five dogs a-barking, four aerialists zooming, three monkeys playing, two elephants, and a daredevil on a high wire.

In the sixth circus ring, my sister saw with me six acrobats, five dogs a-barking, four aerialists zooming, three monkeys playing, two elephants, and a daredevil on a high wire.

In the seventh circus ring, my sister saw with me seven clowns a-clowning, six acrobats, five dogs a-barking, four aerialists zooming, three monkeys playing, two elephants, and a daredevil on a high wire.

In the eighth circus ring, my sister saw with me eight bears performing, seven clowns a-clowning, six acrobats, five dogs a-barking, four aerialists zooming, three monkeys playing, two elephants, and a daredevil on a high wire.

In the ninth circus ring, my sister saw with me nine jugglers juggling, eight bears performing, seven clowns a-clowning, six acrobats, five dogs a-barking, four aerialists zooming, three monkeys playing, two elephants, and a daredevil on a high wire.

In the tenth circus ring, my sister saw with me ten leapers leaping, nine jugglers juggling, eight bears performing, seven clowns a-clowning, six acrobats, five dogs a-barking, four aerialists zooming, three monkeys playing, two elephants, and a daredevil on a high wire.

In the eleventh circus ring, my sister saw with me eleven horseback riders, ten leapers leaping, nine jugglers juggling, eight bears performing, seven clowns a-clowning, six acrobats, five dogs a-barking, four aerialists zooming, three monkeys playing, two elephants, and a daredevil on a high wire.

In the twelfth circus ring, my sister saw with me twelve animals laughing, eleven horseback riders, ten leapers leaping, nine jugglers juggling, eight bears performing, seven clowns a-clowning, six acrobats, five dogs a-barking, four aerialists zooming, three monkeys playing, two elephants, and a daredevil on a high wire.

How many daredevils are there in the circus?
How many elephants can you find?
How many monkeys are monkeying around?
How many dogs are barking in this circus?
How many acrobats can you find?
How many aerialists can you count?
Can you count all of the leapers? How many are there?
How many clowns are clowning around?
How many bears can you find performing in this circus?
How many jugglers are there?
How many horseback riders are riding around?
How many laughing animals can you find in a ring?
How many people and animals are there in the entire circus?
(Hint: begin counting at the first circus ring.)

There is 1 daredevil in each ring of the circus.
1 daredevil x 12 circus rings = 12 daredevils

There are 2 elephants in each of 11 rings.
2 elephants x 11 circus rings = 22 elephants

There are 3 monkeys in each of 10 rings.
3 monkeys x 10 circus rings = 30 monkeys

There are 4 aerialists in 9 rings.
4 aerialists x 9 circus rings = 36 aerialists

There are 5 dogs in 8 rings.
5 dogs x 8 circus rings = 40 dogs

There are 6 acrobats in 7 rings.
6 acrobats x 7 circus rings = 42 acrobats

There are 7 clowns in 6 rings.
7 clowns x 6 rings = 42 clowns
There are the same number of clowns as there are acrobats. Why?

There are 8 bears in 5 rings.
8 bears x 5 rings = 40 bears
There are as many bears as there are dogs. Why?

There are 9 jugglers in 4 rings.
9 jugglers x 4 rings = 36 jugglers
Why are there as many jugglers as there are aerialists

There are 10 leapers in each of 3 rings
10 leapers x 3 rings = 30 leapers
There are as many leapers as there are monkeys. Why?

There are 11 horseback riders in 2 rings.
11 horseback riders x 2 circus rings = 22 horseback riders
There are as many horseback riders as there are elephants. Why?

There are 12 animals laughing in 1 ring.
12 animals x 1 circus ring = 12 animals laughing
There are the same number ot laughing animals as there are daredevils. Why?

There is a total of 364 performers in the circus.

MAKING THE MATH CONNECTION

Have students find the total for each animal or character in the 12 circus rings. Then have them compare methods for finding the totals.

Riddle 14

from *Mother Goose on the Rio Grande*
collected, translated, and arranged by Frances Alexander,
Helen Mar Hunnicutt, Bertha Acevedo, and Hortensia Ramirez

Drawing a picture will help students determine how many birds there are in all. The riddle itself is a tricky one, but letting students turn their drawings into calendars will illustrate the solution.

A tree has twelve branches
With four nests each the same.
Each nest has seven birds,
And each bird has a name.

(Year, months, weeks, and days)

Un árbol con doce ramas;
cada una tiene su nido
cada nido siete pájaros,
y cada cual su apellido.

(El año, los meses, los días de la semana)

BIG BUSINESS

from *Max Malone Makes a Million*
by Charlotte Herman

Max Malone wants to make a million dollars, but none of his get-rich-quick schemes work. When he and his best friend Gordy open a lemonade stand, they find out how important location and variety can be.

"What do we know how to do?" Gordy asked Max.

"Nothing," Max answered.

They were resting on Max's front steps after cleaning up Mrs. Malone's kitchen. Max was trying to figure out where he had gone wrong, and where Anthony Baker had gone right. Maybe Anthony had an older stove. Or a better recipe.

"We'd better think of something fast," said Gordy. "Vacation is over in two weeks."

Max sighed deeply. Then he shut his eyes and tried to think of something he knew how to do. Something he knew about. He knew about garage sales. One of his favorite things to do was to buy lots of great junk at Mrs. Filbert's garage sales. Mrs. Filbert was Max's neighbor. Max and Gordy could have a garage sale. The problem was, Max didn't have a garage. Neither did Gordy.

The door swung open and out came Mrs. Malone with two glasses of lemonade. "Here, boys. I think you can use this."

"Hey, thanks," said Max and Gordy, taking the glasses from her. They gulped down their drinks.

"Boy, this lemonade hits the spot," said Gordy.

"Lemonade!" shouted Max, jumping to his feet. "That's it. We'll make our millions in lemonade."

"Are you kidding? We tried to sell the stuff lots of times. Rosalie drank most of it. She charged it and never paid us back. We didn't make a single penny."

"We weren't running a real business before," said Max. "We were just fooling around. Besides, do you have any better ideas?"

"No," answered Gordy.

"Then we'll sell lemonade," said Max. "It's easy to make. And it's cheap." He could just picture it. First they would sell lemonade from a stand. And when they became real successful, they would go on to big business. They could sell frozen lemonade in a supermarket. Or fresh, in cartons.

The next day Max and Gordy set up their lemonade stand in the park. Max had a pitcher filled with lemonade made from fresh lemons. He had added sugar little by little, until he got it to taste just right. He topped it all off with ice cubes. Gordy brought a small folding table, two chairs, and paper cups. They hung a sign from the table. It read:

LEMONADE
25 cents

"Business should be real good," said Max. "It's going to be a hot day."

They sat down at the table. They tried to look very businesslike while they waited for their first customer.

Soon their first customer was walking toward them. It was Rosalie.

"I'd like to try some of your lemonade," she said.

"That will be twenty-five cents," said Max.

"Charge it," said Rosalie.

"Cash only," said Max.

Rosalie hesitated for a moment. Then she dug into her pocket and came up with a quarter. She plunked it down on the table. Max and Gordy exchanged smiles. They were proud of how businesslike they were acting. Max poured some lemonade into a cup and watched her drink it.

"Just as I thought," she said. "It isn't sweet enough." She turned to leave. "Maybe I'll bring you some more sugar later."

What Max and Gordy needed were more customers. At this rate Max's mother would be selling memo pads forever. "The park is so empty today," said Max.

"Probably because of the heat," said Gordy.

"I sure am thirsty," said Max.

"Me too," said Gordy.

"I've been thinking," said Max. "Maybe we should taste the lemonade again. To see if Rosalie is right about the sugar."

"Good idea," said Gordy. "We don't want to sell sour lemonade."

Each poured himself a cup and drank it down in one gulp.

"It's sweet enough for me," said Max.

"Plenty sweet," said Gordy. "Let's try a little more. Just to be sure."

After the second cup, they waited for more customers. The sun was beating down on them. The ice cubes were beginning to melt. They poured themselves some more lemonade.

"It's only right that we taste it again," said Max. "To see if melted ice cubes affect the flavor."

They drank the lemonade and decided that it was still sweet enough. Then they waited some more.

Finally three small boys followed by their mother ran into the park.

"At last," said Max.

"This is it," said Gordy.

"Hey, lemonade!" the oldest boy shouted.

"Yay, lemonade!" shouted the younger ones. And all three ran toward Max and Gordy.

"An easy seventy-five cents," said Max.

"Maybe even a dollar," said Gordy when he saw the mother coming after her sons.

"We want lemonade," the boys told their mother.

"Not now," she said.

"But we're thirsty."

"We don't know what's in it," she whispered as she led them away.

Max and Gordy were angry. And insulted.

"What does she think is in here, anyway?" asked Max.

"Yeah," said Gordy. "Poison?"

They poured themselves some more lemonade and drank it. They wanted the mother to see them drinking it. She would see that it wasn't poisoned. Besides, they were thirsty. And hot. The ice cubes had melted completely.

"This tastes like sour water," said Max.

"Yeah," said Gordy. "Warm sour water. It's definitely not quality."

"It needs more sugar," said Max.

By the time Rosalie came back with some sugar, Max and Gordy were ready to leave.

"How was business?" asked Rosalie.

"Slow," said Max.

"Too bad," said Rosalie. "Austin is making fortune."

"Austin is selling lemonade?" asked Max.

"Yes. Two kinds. One made with sugar, and one with Sweet 'n Low. Remember when we saw those men chopping up that sidewalk on Friday?" She began adding sugar to the lemonade.

"Yeah," said Max. "In front of the post office."

"Well, today they're pouring cement for the new sidewalk. And that's where Austin is." She sat down at the table and little by little drank up the rest of the lemonade.

They took apart the stand and dropped everything off at Max's house. Then they hurried over to the post office.

Sure enough, there was Austin selling lemonade to three construction workers, who were standing in line. Two ladies coming out of the post office stood behind them to buy lemonade from "that cute little boy."

Max and Gordy exchanged angry glances. This was definitely not fair. Making a million dollars was Max's idea. Not Austin's.

"Hi, guys," Austin called when his customers left. "Want a drink?"

"We're not thirsty," said Max. He could still taste the warm lemonade, which was starting to rise up to his throat. He probably wouldn't touch the stuff for the rest of the summer.

"How's business?" asked Max. He knew the answer even before Austin gave it.

"It's great. I figured I'd get some practice on my own before I'm old enough to join up with you." He poured himself a cup of water and drank it down.

"What's the matter, Austin? asked Gordy. "Don't you trust your lemonade?"

"I don't want to drink up all my profits," Austin answered. "When I'm thirsty, I drink the water. And sell the lemonade."

Max watched the people walking in and out of the post office. He watched the construction workers wiping sweat off their faces. So many people. So many *thirsty* people. Why hadn't he thought to come here?

"You picked a pretty good spot to set up your stand," said Max. He hated to admit it, but it was true.

"Yeah," said Austin. "I knew these men would be here today. I knew they'd be thirsty. You just have to be in the right place at the right time. You've got to know your market. Know your customers. Too bad they won't be here tomorrow. I'll have to figure out something else to do."

Max watched Austin empty the cup of money into his pockets. He could see the quarters, nickels, and dimes pouring out of the cup. He even saw a dollar bill.

"Boy. Making a million dollars sure is fun," said Austin. "I can't wait until tomorrow."

INDEX BY TITLE

Age, 18

Big Business, 62

City Green, 7

Difference, The, 15

8,000 Stones, 43
Enty Merchants, Erith Robbers, 37

Flat Stanley, 16

Garage Sale Fever, 13
Guno's Hunger, 11

I'm Good at Naming, 26
Indians of the Plains Say, 53
It's Hot . . . Really! Treasure of a Desert Park, 27

Kate 'n Toady: Collection Day, 24

Music, Music for Everyone, 19

Nine-in-One, Grr! Grr!, 28
Number of Spots, The, 3

Practicing, 23

Race That Was Rigged, The, 40
Riddle 14, 61

Tom Fox and the Apple Pie, 55
Totem Pole, 54
Twelve Circus Rings, The, 58
Two Foolish Cats, The, 32

Village of Round and Square Houses, The, 47

Young Lions, 1

INDEX OF MATH CONNECTIONS

ADDITION
Age, 18
Difference, The, 15
Enty Merchants, Erith Robbers, 37
Garage Sale Fever, 13
Guno's Hunger, 11
I'm Good at Naming, 26
Number of Spots, The, 3
Tom Fox and the Apple Pie, 55
Young Lions, 1

COUNTING
Guno's Hunger, 11

DIVISION
Age, 18
Big Business, 62
Enty Merchants, Erith Robbers, 37
Nine-in-One, Grr! Grr!, 28
Riddle 14, 61
Tom Fox and the Apple Pie, 55
Twelve Circus Rings, The, 58
Two Foolish Cats, The, 32

ESTIMATING
Big Business, 62
Number of Spots, The, 3

FRACTIONS
Tom Fox and the Apple Pie, 55
Totem Pole, 54

GEOMETRY
Indians of the Plains Say, 53
Village of Round and Square Houses, The, 47

MEASUREMENT
8,000 Stones, 43
Flat Stanley, 16
It's Hot . . . Really! Treasure of a Desert Park, 27
Race That Was Rigged, The, 40

MONEY
Big Business, 61
Difference, The, 15
Garage Sale Fever, 13
Tom Fox and the Apple Pie, 55

MULTIPLICATION
Age, 18
Big Business, 62
Enty Merchants, Erith Robbers, 37
I'm Good at Naming, 26
It's Hot . . . Really! Treasure of a Desert Park, 27
Kate 'n Toady: Collection Day, 24
Nine-in-One, Grr! Grr!, 28
Riddle 14, 61
Twelve Circus Rings, The, 58

NUMBER SENSE
Age, 18
City Green, 7
Enty Merchants, Erith Robbers, 37
Guno's Hunger, 11
Kate 'n Toady: Collection Day, 24
Twelve Circus Rings, The, 58
Young Lions, 1

PATTERNING
Twelve Circus Rings, The, 58

PROBLEM SOLVING
8,000 Stones, 43
Enty Merchants, Erith Robbers, 37
Nine-in-One, Grr! Grr!, 28
Riddle 14, 61

STATISTICS
Music, Music for Everyone, 19
Practicing, 23

SUBTRACTION
Age, 18
Enty Merchants, Erith Robbers, 37
Flat Stanley, 16
Guno's Hunger, 11
Number of Spots, The, 3
Tom Fox and the Apple Pie, 55
Young Lions, 1

TIME
Music, Music for Everyone, 19
Practicing, 23
Riddle 14, 61

INDEX BY AUTHOR

Acevedo, B., 60
Alexander, F., 61

Blair, Lee, 26
Brown, Jeff, 16

Carlson, Bernice Wells, 37
Chwast, Seymour, 58
Courlander, Harold, 11

Davidson, A., 18
DiSalvo-Ryan, DyAnne, 7

Elliot, Geraldine, 3

Greaves, Nick, 40
Grifalconi, Ann, 47

Herman, C., 62
Hoyt-Goldsmith, Diane, 54
Hunnicutt, H., 61

Jacobs, Allan and Leland, 15

Liatsos, Sandra, 23

Myers, Laurie, 13

Ramirez, H., 61
Rinard, Judith E., 27
Rovetch, Lissa, 24

Spagnoli, Cathy, 28

Uchida, Yoshiko, 32

Watson, Clyde, 55
Williams, Vera B., 19
Wolkstein, Diane, 43
Wood, Flora, 53

Xiong, Blia, 28

Yoshida, Toshi, 1

INDEX OF CULTURAL CONNECTIONS

AFRICA
Number of Spots, The, 3
Race That Was Rigged, The, 40
Village of Round and Square Houses, The, 47

CHINA
8,000 Stones, 43

INDIA
Enty Merchants, Erith Robbers, 37

INDONESIA
Guno's Hunger, 11

JAPAN
Two Foolish Cats, The, 32

LAOS
Nine-in-One, Grr! Grr!, 28

MEXICO
Riddle 14, 61

NATIVE AMERICA
Indians of the Plains Say, 53
Totem Pole, 54

INDEX OF SELECTIONS BY CONTINENT

AFRICA

Number of Spots, The, 3
Retold by Geraldine Elliot

Race That Was Rigged, The, 40
Told by Nick Greaves

Village of Round and Square Houses, The, 47
By Ann Grifalconi

ASIA

China
8,000 Stones, 43
Retold by Diane Wolkstein

India
Enty Merchants, Erith Robbers, 37
By Bernice Wells Carlson

Indonesia
Guno's Hunger, 11
Retold by Harold Courlander

Japan
Two Foolish Cats, The, 32
Retold by Yoshiko Uchida

Laos
Nine-in-One, Grr! Grr!, 28
Told by Blia Xiong, adapted by Cathy Spagnoli

NORTH AMERICA

Age, 18
By Avelyn Davidson

Big Business, 62
By Charlotte Herman

City Green, 7
By DyAnne DiSalvo-Ryan

Difference, The, 15
Selected by Allan and Leland Jacobs

Garage Sale Fever, 13
By Laurie Myers

I'm Good at Naming, 26
By Lee Blair

Indians of the Plains Say, 53
Selected by Flora Hood

It's Hot . . . Really! Treasure of a Desert Park, 27
By Judith E. Rinard

Kate 'n Toady: Collection Day, 24
By Lissa Rovetch

Music, Music for Everyone, 19
By Vera B. Williams

Practicing, 23
By Sandra Liatsos

Riddle 14, 61
Selected by F. Alexander, H. Hunnicut, B. Acevedo, H. Ramirez

Tom Fox and the Apple Pie, 55
By Clyde Watson

Totem Pole, 54
By Diane Hoyt-Goldsmith

Twelve Circus Rings, The, 58
By Seymour Chwast

Young Lions, 1
By Toshi Yoshida

INDEX BY CATEGORY

STORIES
Big Business, 62

8,000 Stones, 43
Enty Merchants, Erith Robbers, 37

Flat Stanley, 16

Garage Sale Fever, 13
Guno's Hunger, 11

Kate n' Toady: Collection Day, 24

Music, Music for Everyone, 19

Nine-in-One, Grr! Grr!, 28
Number of Spots, The, 3

Race That Was Rigged, The, 40

Tom Fox and the Apple Pie, 55
Twelve Circus Rings, The, 58
Two Foolish Cats, The, 32

Village of Round and Square Houses, The, 47

Young Lions, 1

POEMS
Age, 18

Difference, The, 15

I'm Good at Naming, 26
Indians of the Plains Say, 53

Practicing, 23

Riddle 14, 61

NONFICTION
City Green, 7

It's Hot . . . Really! Treasure of a Desert Park, 27

Totem Pole, 54

ACKNOWLEDGMENTS

(continued from page iii)

"The Number of Spots" from the LONG GRASS WHISPERS by Geraldine Elliot. Copyright © 1939 by Geraldine Elliot. Reprinted by permission of Laurence Pollinger Limited.

"Practicing" by Sandra Liatsos. Copyright © 1993 by Sandra Liatsos. Used by permission of Marian Reiner for the author.

"The Race That Was Rigged" from WHEN HIPPO WAS HAIRY AND OTHER TALES FROM AFRICA by Nick Greaves. Copyright © 1988 by Nick Greaves. Reprinted by arrangement with Barron's Educational Series, Inc., Hauppauge, New York.

"Riddle 14" from MOTHER GOOSE ON THE RIO GRANDE: *Mexican Folklore* collected, translated and arranged by Frances Alexander et al. Copyright © 1944 by Banks Upshaw and Company. Reprinted by permission of NTC Publishing, 4255 W. Touhy Avenue, Lincolnwood, IL 60646.

TOM FOX AND THE APPLE PIE by Clyde Watson. Copyright © 1972 by Clyde Watson. Published by Harper & Row. Reprinted by permission of Curtis Brown, Ltd.

Excerpt from TOTEM POLE by Diane Hoyt-Goldsmith. Copyright © 1990 by Diane Hoyt-Goldsmith. Reprinted by arrangement with Holiday House, New York.

Text from THE TWELVE CIRCUS RINGS by Seymour Chwast. Copyright © 1993 by Seymour Chwast. Reprinted by permission of Harcourt Brace & Company.

THE TWO FOOLISH CATS by Yoshiko Uchida. Text copyright © 1986 by Yoshiko Uchida. Reprinted with permission of Margaret K. McElderry Books, an imprint of Simon & Schuster Children's Publishing Division.

Excerpt from THE VILLAGE OF ROUND AND SQUARE HOUSES by Ann Grifalconi. Copyright © 1986 by Ann Grifalconi. By permission of Little, Brown and Company.

Excerpt from YOUNG LIONS by Toshi Yoshida. Copyright © 1982 by Toshi Yoshida. American text copyright © 1989 by Philomel Books. Reprinted with permission of Philomel Books.

Cover Design: © 1993 Kevin Schafer
Page vii Illustration: Marsha Slomowitz
Pages 24 & 25 Illustrations: Lissa Rovetch
All Other Illustrations: Laura Coyle